Printed
For
Quixote Press
by
BRENNAN PRINTING
100 Main Street
Deep River, Iowa 52222
515-595-2000

SKUNK RIVER ANTHOLOGY

by

Gene "Will" Olson

QUIXOTE PRESS
R.R. #4, Box 33B
Blvd. Station
Sioux City, Iowa 51109

* * * * * * * * * * * *

QUIXOTE
PRESS
Bruce Carlson
R.R. *#4, Box 33B*
Blvd. Station
Sioux City, Iowa
51109

PRINTED IN U.S.A.

Some of these stories could cause embarrassment to living people today. Because of that, some of the stories use fictitious names. In those cases, it should be understood that any similarity between those names and actual persons, living or dead, is purely coincidental.

DEDICATION

To my loving wife, Lois Elaine, who laughed and cried over my scribblings and thus encouraged me to prevail. She did not live to see these few stories published in this book but said over and over, they were very worthy.

TABLE OF CONTENTS

FOREWORD 9

PREFACE 11

CHAPTERS

I AN IMPRESSIONABLE AGE 13

II THE FRUITS OF WHOSE LABOR? 19

III AXEL'S FREE LIGHT POLE 23

IV BLEMISHED JUDGMENT 35

V DOC DALE 51

VI HOW NOT TO CATCH A GROUNDHOG 61

VII WATERMELON TIME 69

VIII THE PRIDE OF ANDER AND SIGNA 77

IX HE BEARS WATCHIN' 113

X ALVIN JUNK 117

XI A CURE FOR THE COMMON COLD 125

XII THE SHOOTING OF BUCK HENSHAW 133

XIII PROBLEMS WITH THE TELEPHONE 139

XIV THE HOMECOMING 147

EPILOGUE 151

FOREWORD

The Skunk River certainly isn't one of Iowa's best known rivers. And Will Olson's folks he writes about in SKUNK RIVER ANTHOLOGY are not the most famous of Iowa's people.

But, how much more Iowa can you get than that beautiful Skunk River with the kind of silly name? How much more Iowa can you get than folks watchin' the family dog chase a rabbit, young bucks chasing girls, and old men chasing memories of life in early Iowa?

Yet today, here in Iowa, we have some viperish little ankle-chewin' lap dogs, dang clever ground hogs, and guys that have reason to wish they'd bought a cheaper grade of overalls.

If you're looking for a book that's worth the money, you're holding one right now.

Prof. Phil Hey
Briar Cliff College
Sioux City, Ia.

PREFACE

This book isn't about anyone you'd know or read about in any newspaper or magazine article. It's just about some of the folks I crossed paths with while growin' up and livin' as a young man in the Skunk River Valley In Iowa.

If you're looking for names to drop at parties and all you won't find them here. The most excitement these folks caused was maybe a little ruckus on goin'-to-town night or something like that. Of course, the day Buck Henshaw got shot was pretty heady stuff. Well, okay, he didn't actually get shot, but he might as well have for all the ruckus he raised about it.

CHAPTER I

AN IMPRESSIONABLE AGE

Mother never liked Pa's drinking. I guess you couldn't blame her, in a way. But, then, Pa never hurt anyone with it. On the contrary, you might say he helped quite a few folks. He always laughed, joked, and pulled capers of a harmless type.

To him, and whoever happened to be with him, it was just a lot of damn fun.

A time or two, I'd overheard the neighbors make remarks like . . .

"Ya know, if I could drink and have half the fun that Harry does, I'd take it up right away."

Of course, there were times when he'd get "carried away" and forget to come home in time to do the evening chores. Then Mother and I would have to do them ourselves.

We didn't appreciate that chore-doin' too much, but you could be sure of one thing. When he drank, everything was running pretty smooth and we were secure. If things weren't that way, he wouldn't take a drink until they were.

I was thirteen, an age when a boy eyes his parents pretty closely. One thing I didn't have nailed down, yet, for real sure, was which one was the absolute "boss".

One evening when I was gettin' back from school, Mother said; "Will, you'd better get the cows in from the pasture a little early tonight, we might have to do the chores ourselves. Your Pa took some hogs to town to sell. If he gets a good price, he might forget to come home."

So, we fed the cattle, did the milking and slopped the remaining hogs. Sure enough, darkness came and no Pa. About ten o'clock I went upstairs to bed.

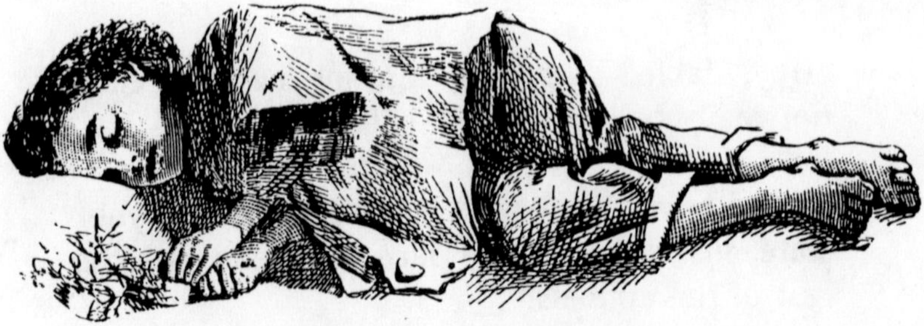

I had just barely gotten to sleep when I woke up and heard our old Ford truck pull in the driveway. It wasn't hard to tell that it was Pa in his cups. He always forgot the stock rack was on the truck and he'd try to drive into the garage.

The door was too low to let that rack clear. It caught the top and I could hear the wood cracking and creaking as the truck ground to a stop.

Pa shut the motor off and kind of worked his way to the house. Every once in a while I'd hear him through the window chuckling to himself, probably thinking about something that someone said or did at Murphy's Tavern.

He came around to the back door and tried the latch a time or two. Mother had the door locked!

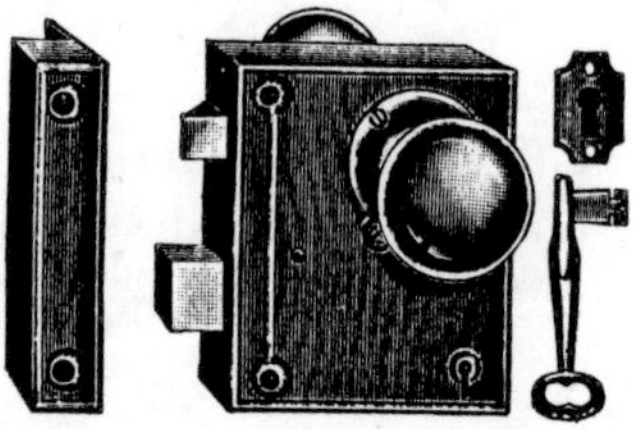

"Hey, Mable!! Ya got the door locked?" he called not really believing such a thing could be.

"Yes, I have! You're not coming in here in your state. Just go out to the barn and sleep with the rest of the animals!"

Pa muttered something I couldn't make out. I lay with my hands behind my head and listened. "Sleep in the barn!" I thought, "Boy, oh boy, Ma's really laying the law down to him this time!"

We had a weighted walk-through gate that separated the house yard from the barnyard. When it swung open, its dry hinges made a squawking sound. I heard it squawk and then heard the whap-ra-rap-rap as it banged shut against the stop post.

I thought, "Dang, he's actually gonna go to the barn!" I felt a little ashamed, and had kind of a sinkin' feeling. I figured he'd put up more of a fight than that. But then, Ma was a pretty hard-boiled old gal, and she had her dander up.

After a minute or two, I heard the gate squawk again, "What the . . . . ., he's comin' back?"

I hardly had time to think, when the whole house shook, and the lamps got to rattlin' and shakin'.

I leaped out of bed, bounding down the stairs two or three at a time.

There laid Pa on the kitchen floor, his arms still wrapped around the hedge fence post he'd used for a battering ram. The door hung all slaunch-wise by one hinge, the panels shattered. Ma stood with her hands on her hips, speechless.

Pa got to his feet and said, "Dammit, Mable, Ya don't lock a man out of his own house!"

Pa walked a bit unsteadily past me, into their bedroom, and dropped into bed, and fell asleep immediately.

I ain't gonna say what Ma said. I just went on up to bed. Slept good, too!

CHAPTER II

THE FRUITS OF WHOSE LABOR?

Our house stood at the edge of a small town, on a five-acre tract of pretty level pasture.

I had just gotten done cutting brush from the fence lines around the edge of the place, piling the limbs in several small piles here and there.

As I leaned on the fence visiting with my next-door neighbor, Jack Bewely, my half shepherd dog kicked a rabbit up from Jack's garden and with excited yips, he chased it through a gate into the open pasture. That rabbit made for the nearest brush pile with old Ted in hot pursuit.

Our conversation barely missed a beat over this unimportant event, though our eyes followed the chase.

Ted scouted around the small brush pile, finally making that dog-food-on-the-hoof nervous enough to risk finding better cover, and the race was on to the next brush pile, where the whole thing was repeated.

Now, Jack had an old decrepit 'an broken down bulldog named Snip who spent a great deal of time sleeping. He'd given up chasing rabbits as a hopeless job. However, the sport still interested him enough that he was more than willing to be a spectator.

Ted's excited yapping as he pursued the rabbit from one brush pile to another woke Snip up from his nap. He got stiffly to his feet, yawned, gave a halfhearted stretch and wandered on out by the gate where Jack and I stood.

Snip's old eyes, dimmed by age didn't let him enjoy the sight of the contest, but his ears followed the sounds of the chase as it went around the pasture.

The cottontail, at last, decided there was no safe place in these skinny brush piles, so he elected to come back into the heavy foliaged garden where it had all begun.

Ted, still in hot, tongue-lolling pursuit, and run-ning the rabbit for all he was worth, laid on an extra spurt of speed, hoping to end the contest in the last fifty yards of open pasture before his prey could get himself hidden in the garden.

Bounding through the same gateway she had come out of just minutes before, the luckless rabbit was snapped up in the waiting jaws of worn-out old Snip, who had hardly found it necessary to raise from his relaxed half-sitting position.

Ted skidded to a stop to keep from running into Snip as the old bulldog limped off with the still-kicking rabbit clamped in his time-worn stumps of teeth.

Ted sat down for a badly needed rest, with his tongue lolling over the side of his mouth and saliva dripping off the end, intently watching Snip limp toward his dog house.

Then he glanced up at Jack and me with an expression in his eyes that seemed to say, "Well, Snip's got it, but there's something not quite right about this whole deal!"

CHAPTER III

AXEL'S FREE LIGHT POLE

In our rural community we had a scrooge, a different type than the classic example we all know about, but a scrooge nevertheless.

Axel Carlson was a real "well-to-do" farmer, although you'd never guess it by his appearance or the way he lived and made his family work. He'd accumulated his hoard by bein' tighter'n the bark on a tree, and he meant to keep

it that way. The only entertainment he allowed himself and his family was goin' to church Sunday mornings.

Axel Carlson was a bald fellow, ruggedly built, with deep-set piercing blue eyes. He'd done a lot of hard work in his day; in fact, he was the type that if there was a hard way to do a job, that's the way he'd do it.

Axel didn't neighbor or trade help with anyone. He didn't need to; he had three big strapping boys, fair-haired and strong as oxen. He ruled them with an iron fist and brainwashed them by constantly preaching that the only place was home and the best remedy for all ills was hard work. He'd done a good job; they were his slaves.

Pa had mowed down twenty acres of clover hay. It was to be the main feed for our milk cows through the coming winter. The hay had dried a day or two and Pa was raking it into long windrows, gettin' ready to bale it.

At dinner time, the radio told us that a storm front was moving our way. Rain was forecast. If it rained before we got the hay in the barn, it meant very poor quality feed. If the storm were to last a long time, maybe we wouldn't get any hay at all.

Our nearest neighbors were in the same fix. When it's haying time for one, it's usually haying time for everyone.

Axel, however, had his hay in. I heard Pa tell Mother that as much as he hated to, he was going to ask Axel if he could hire a couple of his boys for a day or two. I was a young lad at the time, old enough to drive a tractor, but not big enough to handle the heavy bales.

I rode with Pa over to the Carlson place. When we pulled into the driveway, two of the boys were in the barn, working on a tractor. They didn't greet us, just looked up toward the house as Axel came out to see what we wanted. Company was a tad scarce, but when somebody did come, Axel did all the talking. It wasn't the boys' place to leave their work for idle talk with neighbors.

Pa explained his situation and asked if he might hire two of the boys.

"I'll pay 'em good; I'm not askin' for favors or to trade help back. I'll pay 'em in cash!"

Axel hooked his thumbs in his suspenders, nodded his head and answered in broken Swedish.

"Oh, ya, the boys, dey vill halp ya, shore. But you don't pay dem, you pay me! If you pay dem, den dey don't work for me anymore. I don't vant my boys ruined. You don't say nothin' to dem 'bout pay, you yust pay me!"

So, that's the way it was done. Pa didn't like it. Axel was a tyrant, a successful tyrant, and that didn't set too good with Pa.

Some time later at church when the collection plate was passed, Pa saw Axel put a five-dollar bill in the plate and take out four ones. This, of course, was unethical. No one took money out of the collection plate. If you were in church and discovered all you had was a five or a ten, you just put it in.

But, that's not the way Axel figured it.

Pa didn't like Axel at all, really. So, later, in telling some of the neighbors about the collection plate incident, he made it a little worse than it really was. He hinted that he didn't actually "see" Axel put the five in, but he did see him take the four out. Knowing Axel as they did, it kind of left them smiling and rubbing their jaws in thought.

Pa used to do some drinking with a tall, skinny, yellow-complexioned bachelor by the name of Fred Martinson.

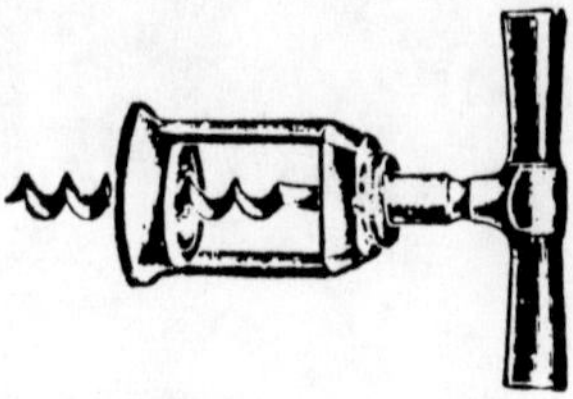

Fred was a slow mover and real dry with his humor. Pa was just the opposite. I guess that's why they got along so well.

Fred drove a 1926 Model T Ford sedan. It was antique to everyone but Fred. To him it was gettin'-around real slow-like which was exactly what he wanted. Fred never drove over fifteen or twenty miles an hour.

If he was drinkin' he drove even slower than that.

Fred carefully guided the T into out driveway one Sunday afternoon. He had a jug and while he and Pa visited and passed the jug back and forth, I kind of slinked around listening, mostly 'cause I didn't have anything else to do.

Pretty soon I heard Fred come up with an idea about what they should do. He told Pa the two of them ought to go back to his place where they could tap another jug.

"This here jug's about empty. We oughta' git on over to my place and git us another 'un before we run out, don't ya know?"

The idea dawned on me to sneak a ride with them. "Hard Luck" Hansson lived across the road from Fred. He had a boy, Carl, my age and I figured that while Pa and Fred sat 'round drinkin' and tellin' stories, Carl and I could have a couple hours of playin' and messin' around.

I knew that if I asked Pa if I could go along, he'd say no. He didn't want me along listening to their bull and rough talk.

I got around on the other side of the T, opened the rear door real quietly and crawled in to lay down on the floor behind the front seat.

Both Pa and Fred were feeling pretty good by then. They got in the front seat and we were off. I figured if we got far enough down the road before they discovered me, there would be nothing they could do but let me go with them the rest of the way.

We chugged along about ten miles an hour. Pa and Fred laughed and carried on like a couple of kids. After a while Pa said, "Say, Fred, who's that up the road there?"

Fred peered out the windshield, "It looks like Axel Carlson."

"By Golly!, you're right. It is Axel. What's he doin' down in the ditch? Why, he's got a pole! By God, he's stealing a light pole, that's what he's doin'!"

Pa's tone of voice got my curiosity all riled up 'til I couldn't stay down any longer. I had to see what was goin' on.

I raised up real quiet like and sat on my knees on the back seat.

You see, the electric company was replacing their light poles along that road. The old ones were

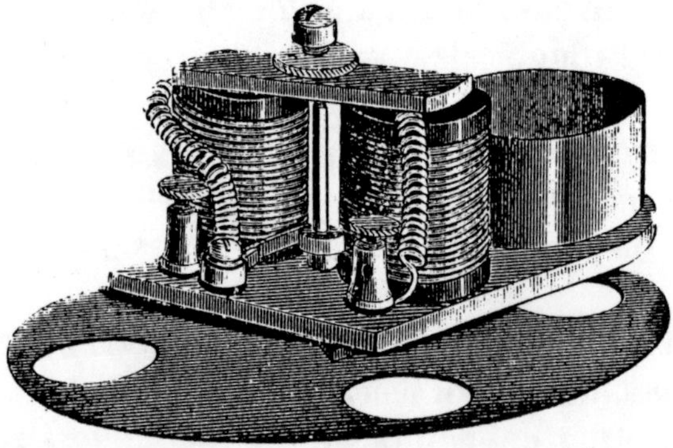

showin' signs of rot and they'd just drop off new ones every bit of a spell along in that ditch. A crew would be comin' along later to set those poles.

Axel had seen his chance to get a new barnyard light pole. He'd just carry one in, hide it behind the barn and when the power company was done and out of the area, he'd have his boys set it and change the wires over from the old pole. Axel figured there was no need to be spending good money when the light company likely had more poles than they knew what to do with, anyhow.

The road past his place was usually pretty deserted on Sunday afternoons. Axel musta' figured he could get one carried in before anyone happened by.

The pole was about twenty-five feet long, all tarred up, and heavy as all get out; 'most too heavy for one man to handle.

But, old Axel had one end up on his shoulder and was working his way toward the middle. If he could get it balanced on his shoulder just right, he should be able to carry it the short distance to his driveway.

As we got closer to Axel, he got it balanced and was staggering out onto the edge of the road. The ends of the pole rose and fell in slow motion, timed to Axel's slow and measured tread.

"Lookit that thievin' old cuss! On Sunday, too! Pull over close to him and slow down, Fred. I wanta say hello as we go by."

Fred slowed to a crawl. Pa opened the car door up and sat on the edge of the seat with his feet on the running board. As we chugged past Axel, Pa said, "Good afternoon, Mr. Carlson."

Axel didn't dare turn his head to see who greeted him, the balance of the pole was too delicate. Any distraction might foul his concentration. He just rolled his eyes sideways and grunted, "Uh huh."

As we passed the end of the pole, Pa reached out with his foot and gave it a light kick.

I watched out the back window as we chugged on down the road. Slowly, that pole started its sweeping arc, forcing Axel to turn with it. He fought to retain the balance, trying desperately to stop the ponderous sweep. He turned completely around once. Still he kept his shaky hold. Truly, this man had grit!

On the second revolution, his knees buckled a bit,

his face and ears red with the strain. He staggered back a step, stumbled forward with a jerk, then slipped sideways off the shoulder of the road and tumbled down in the ditch with the pole on top of him. A considerable amount of dust rose up out of the ditch as we disappeared over the top of the hill.

Pa had been watching, too, of course. As Axel disappeared out of sight, Pa said to Fred, "Ya know, I probably ought to stay out of Axel's way for awhile."

CHAPTER IV

BLEMISHED JUDGMENT

It'd been a long day. I'd opened our tavern/grocery/store at eight that morning and worked straight through 'cept for an hour break at noon and supper time when my wife interrupted her housework so's I could go upstairs to eat and take a short nap if I wanted. Our little town business wasn't all that rushing, but it did call for you being on your feet most of the time.

'Long about eleven o'clock it looked like the night's traffic wasn't gonna be too hectic, and I'd likely be able to close a bit earlier than usual.

I opened a beer and kept one there with me at the cash register during the rest of the hour. By midnight most of my customers had drifted away and home to bed. The only ones still around were two brothers, Bobby Joe and Cliff Enlminger.

Those two loafers each had about half a bottle of beer to finish, so while they leaned their long six-foot frames across a table just visitin', I turned out the front lights, locked the back door, and counted out the day's proceeds. I always counted the money out before sticking it in the safe for the night.

Bobby Joe and Cliff were two of my closest friends, and the three of us had done a lot of fishing, hunting, and general carousing around together.

The brothers were about half "hooked up", having spent most of the evening visitin' and drinkin' beer, all mixed up with an occasional game of pool.

I had a slight glow on myself from the three or four beers I'd had so I reached down in the cooler to get a twelve pack.

"Ya know, fellas, I've been cooped up in this place long enough. Whadda-ya-say we go out on the front steps an' drink a leisurely beer or two so's I can get some fresh air?"

"Sounds like a fine idea, Will," Bobby agreed. "I'll bet it does git tiresome havin' to stay in here so many hours when the weather's as nice as it is."

I locked the front door behind us and we sprawled out on the second step, leaning back there on the first one.

A nice breeze had sprung up from the south, and it felt mighty good. The town was quiet except for an occasional passing car and the yappin' of a dog on the other side of town. Across the street in a big old soft maple tree, a locust was singing its song. These kinds of sounds were not what you'd call aggravating, but were sounds of peace and tranquility.

We sat visiting in low tones, swapping lies and making plans for an all-night "trotline" fishing excursion on the Skunk River the next time it rained enough to get the fish to start feedin'.

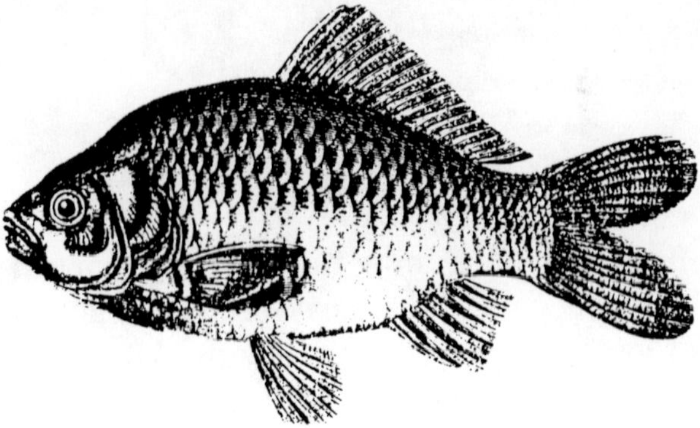

The contents of the twelve pack took its toll and pretty soon Cliff got up and stepped around the corner of the store, out of the glare from the street light to do his thing.

Cliff's eyes got kind of used to the darkness and he noticed a bicycle leaning again the wall. Bending down for a closer look, he asked, "Hey, Will, who's homemade miscarriage of a motorbike is this?"

I leaned over, peering around the corner, trying to figure out what he was talking about when I realized what it was.

"Oh, I'll bet that's Kent Mills' contraption. I seen him ride it into town today. I think he got in a car with some of his buddies and just left it there. Probably be after it come morning."

Cliff shoved it out under the street light so's to get a better look at it. It was an ordinary bicycle except for the altering Kent had done to it. He'd sawed the frame in two and welded twelve-inch lengths of pipe in to lengthen the wheel base to make room for a one-cylinder Briggs and Stratton engine.

The motor was mounted below and just ahead of the seat with a V-belt running back to the rear wheel. The pedal arms were welded solid at the half-turn position to serve as foot rests. This eliminated the conventional bicycle brakes, of course.

Bobby and I walked over to give the machine a closer look, our curosity being worked up 'bout this time.

Kent was just a kid, but known to be mechanically inclined and bordering on being a genious when it came to cobbling up labor-saving devices and modes of transportation to and from his parents' farm. His pa kept a fully equipped machine shop for fixin' his farm machinery, so Kent had lots of good tools to use.

The thing lacked several finishing touches, which was not surprising in such a young lad. They tire of a project rather quickly, so when Kent had it running well enough, he decided to jus' forget the few remaining details.

Cliff had it leaning against his legs as he bent over the machine to examine the workmanship.

"How the hell does he start it? I dont see any crank or starter rope. There ain't no throttle either, 'cept this piece of balin' wire hangin' down."

"When I seen him ridin' it this morning, he was guidin' it with one hand and workin' the throttle with the other'n by reachin' down and pullin' on that wire. When he wants to stop, he jus' let go the wire an' the compression of the motor stops the thing. Must have purty good compression, too, 'cause it slowed down damn quick."

Cliff nooded, "Uh huh, yeah, see. An' when he starts it he runs 'long side pushin' 'til the belt turns the motor over fast enough, huh?"

"Yeah," I agreed. "That's it."

We were feeling our beer pretty strong now, otherwise I doubt if we'd been so intrigued with the machine. My recuperation from the long day's work seemed about complete, and I'll have to admit that the thought of tryin' the bike out crossed my mind a time or two.

Cliff unscrewed the gas tank cap and peered down in.

"If there's any gas in the . . . yeah, 'most full. Git on 'er, Bob; take it for a trial run. I'll give ya a shove, see if we kin get it started."

Bobby took a step or two backwards.

"Nosiree, I never was worth a damn ridin' a bike, even the ones ya peddled. Seems like I was always top heavy an' too long-legged, 'er somethin'."

Then I chimed in, "I used to be a purty good bike rider. If you'll git on the han'lebars, Bobby, I'll do the runnin' of it."

Bob thought that sounded like a fair deal. So with Cliff steadying it, Bob straddled the front wheel and lifted himself up backwards, settin' on the handlebars with his long legs hanging down barely clearing the ground. I mounted the seat and got set. Cliff said, "Are ya ready?"

"Sure 'nuf, turn this bird loose," I answered, feeling cocksure and ready for a thrill.

Cliff moved around behind to push on the back of the seat and started us going at a fast trot. The motor wheezed and coughed, fired a time or two, then fell back to wheezing a while, fired again, caught and we were under way. Cliff let loose, calling after us, "You're on yer own!"

My first impression was of disappointment. The little motor didn't seem to have much power. Of course, there was Bob at two hundred pounds and myself at one hundred and fifty, so I guess you couldn't expect too much. Pop . . . pop . . . pop. I turned the corner, heading down Elm Street, wobbling quite a bit due to the low speed, and trying to miss the deepest of the chuck holes and largest rocks there on the graveled surface.

Elm Street was seven blocks long. The first four were on a gentle downgrade, then two blocks of light upgrade where it leveled off onto a country road and continued out across country.

As we headed downhill, things started picking up a bit. Pop . . . pop . . . pop.

"Will, I think we're gonna hafta ta git off an' carry this damn thing. She ain't got no stomach for hauling men," Bob threw back at me.

Pop . . . pop . . . pop.

"Yeah, it seems purty week-kneed, Bobby, 'less he's got the belt pulleys fixed so's it won't lug an' has to git wound up to have any power."

I had to holler louder now to make him hear. The engine "pops" were gettin' closer together now, and in less time than it takes to tell it, we were making headway.

I was having trouble seeing around Bobby's bulk on the handlebars. I glanced down at the front wheel and took rather grim notice at how fast the rocks were whipping by beneath us. Bobby noticed that from his perch up there on the handlebars 'cause he tightened his grip and ventured no more talk. Our speed was increasing jus' awful fast, and he apparently seemed satisfied to reflect on that fact in silence.

We were near the bottom of the grade now and starting up the gradual incline. That should cool the little engine down some, I figured. Not so! That dang mighty mite had its dander up now and jus' kept pouring it on.

"Hold yer feet out, Bob! Don't let 'em get hung up in the spokes! If we go down in this gravel, there won't be 'nough skin left to start a graft with!"

"Slack off on the throttle, Will! This damn hog ain' showin' any signs of toppin' out!"

I had to let loose of the handlebar with one hand to reach down under the seat for the balin' wire. This got us all wobbly, but I held on, just 'a clenchin' my teeth til they hurt. Finding the wire, I felt along it and discovered the end of it tangled in the springs of the seat!

"Oh, $!*#%$!. That $#*%$# Kent tied the throttle wide open!"

I had to yell louder now. The wind was whistling in our ears and the motor was rapping out to a high-pitched scream. I couldn't figure why the governor didn't cut in and set it back some. Surely, the governor. . . . . . ! Oh, no! A recollection shot through my mind. Kent had taken the governor out or had unhooked it. Not only that, but he had likely bored out, ported and relieved every damn thing he could to make a wild beast out of that little engine.

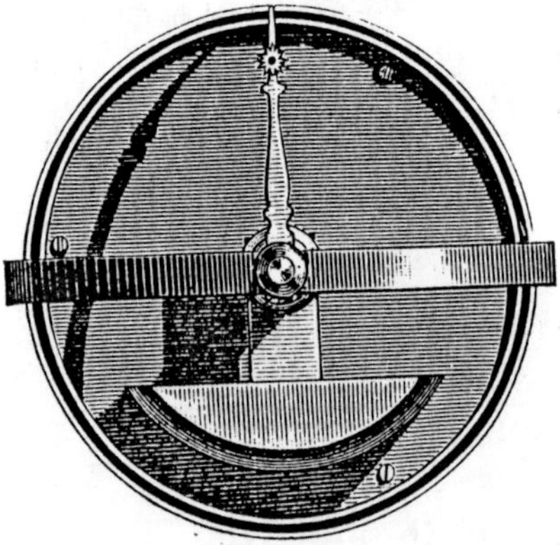

We were nearing the top of the grade and gaining all the time. This monster had to be dumped somewhere or we'd have to ride it out across the prairie God knew how far until it ran out of gas or threw us.

Bobby hollered over his shoulder, "We gotta dump this boar hog some place, Will! $#&?!#$ that Kent anyhow!"

"I know, I bin ready to turn loose of it fer some time now, an' I'm gonna do it, too, first chance I git!"

As we topped the rise, we would soon pass the old abandoned country schoolhouse and grounds. The grass and weeds had not been mowed along the road side and banks for several years. It looked like a good place to dump the runaway and give us a landing place far better than the gravel.

"Git ready, Bob. I'm gonna dump 'er in the schoolyard ditch. That long grass looks purty good."

"Head 'er in, Will, I've had enough of this pie!"

I slanted toward that ditch. The front wheel dropped off the edge, hit something solid and rared up, somersaulting Bob up on the side of the bank in the grass and weeds.

I stayed more with the bike, not having such an unobstructed flight path as he did. Also, enough, so I was flipped over the front in a short arch, like a slingshot, landing in what felt like a bear trap.

I didn't try to move. I jus'lay there feeling the pain spreadin' through me from head to toe.

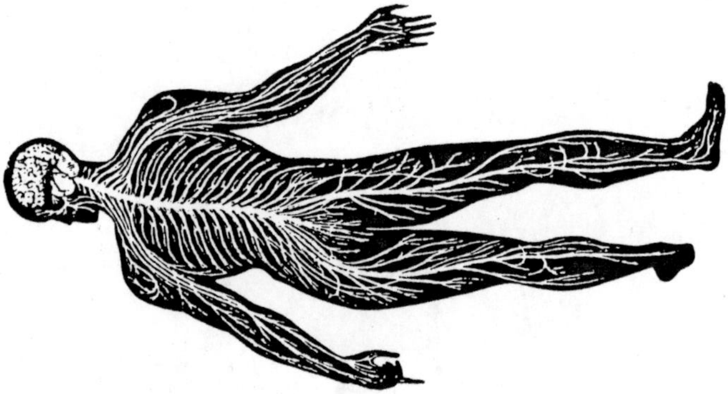

Bobby picked himself up, happily commenting that he hardly had a bruise.

"Ya alright, Will?".

I sucked in a breath, gritting my teeth from the pain in my rib cage.

"No, I sure as hell ain't! I went all to smash on somethin' here. Don't know what it is, but it feels like an iron pile."

Bobby came down the bank, feeling around and helping untangle me from between some steel arms.

"Well, for jumpin' up all get out! I know what this is. It's the frame of the ol' merry-go-round' used to be in the school yard. It wore out years ago an' got throwed out here in the ditch, and got growed over. I fergot it was here."

"Well, the damn thing had one more ride in it, and it was a doozy, too!"

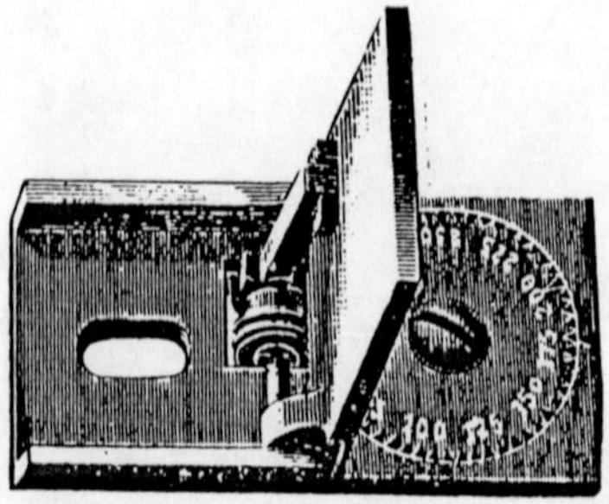

The mechanical wonder lay on its side, the front wheel bent double and a couple of parts layin' 'round. The engine was huffin' and puffin', an' scratchin' with the rear wheel. We climbed out of the ditch up on the side of the road and stood looking down at it with respectful disinterest. Finally, it belched and wheezed its last as blue smoke curled up from the manifold.

After examining myself, I figured out that the only broken bones I had were a couple ribs, and a cartilage or two torn loose, plus a whole lot of bruises, of course.

As we started on our hike back to town, Bobby looked back over his shoulder at the smoking remains.

"Ya know, will that damn Mills kid an' his tinkering is a menace. He ought'n be 'llowed to ride a thing like that into town. It's got no license, no brakes, no light, or nuttin'. A thing like that's dangerous. When he comes to git it tomorrow, tell 'em he better keep it out home. I'm the mayor an' you're on the Council, so tell 'im we're gonna make it bad for 'im if he rides it inside the city limits again."

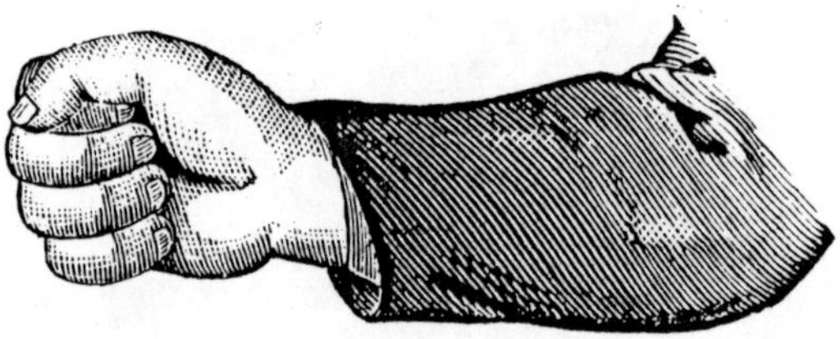

"Ah, to hell with 'im. All I'm gonna tell 'im is where he can find it. I sure ain' gonna have anymore to do with it. Let 'im fix it up and ride it. That's the only way we might get even. He might break his neck on it."

"Yeah, maybe you're right. We'll give the kid some slack; he's bound to pile it up sooner 'er later an' git his reward. In the meantime, I'm gonna figure out a way to git even with that ornery brother of mine."

Bobby's brother, Cliff, was gone when we got back. I didn't much care. He was too big for me to punish. All I could do was to give him a good cussin' out, and the way my breathing was hampered, I couldn't even do a good job of that.

CHAPTER V

DOC DALE

Bein' two years out of high school and newly married with little experience except in farming, Pa offered me the chance of joinin' him in a father-son partnership.

Pa's farm wasn't big enough to afford such an arrangement, so he sold the hundred acres he had and bought a two-hundred and forty acre spread some ninety miles away in Henry County, Iowa.

After moving the machinery, livestock, and so forth, 'en gettin' settled in, our next job was to find the fuel and feed suppliers in our new community.

An' since we were mainly inta dairy and raisin' butcher hogs, we'd need a good veterinarian. A neighbor recommended a Dr. Dale Varhveen. So, while in town one day, Pa called at his office and introduced himself.

After Pa explained about our operation and how we'd be needing his services should the occasion arise, Dr. Varhveen agreed at once to do that.

Dr. Varhveen was sixtyish, some few years older than Pa. He was a slow, steady, and methodical sort of fellow, and unexciteable since he'd been in the veterinary game for many, many years. There was an unusual twinkle in his grey eyes that belied his seeming boredom with his chosen profession.

I never, in all the years we had him take care of our stock, saw him smile. He carried his tall frame straight as a poker and kept a like expression on his face.

Not too long after our first meeting, one of our Holsteins began dropping off feed and milk production. We watched her closely a day or two, noticing she kind of grunted and hunched up when

forced to move above a slow walk. We locked her in a box stall and with the use of nose tongs, snubbed her to a post and "drenched" her with a quart of Epson Salts. This was about the only home cure Pa ever used. The next day she was down and refused to get up. We called Doc Dale.

When he pulled into the driveway, we left our unfinished morning chores to show him to the stall and the listless bovine. Doc stood with hands on his hips studying the sick animal and nodding as we answered his questions.

"When'd ya first notice her off feed? All the rest of the herd awright? How long she been down?"

He stuck a thermometer in her, walked around, stopping by her rear flank and shoving his index finger knuckle into the side of her lower abdomen. The cow switched her tail and moaned. Extracting the thermometer and holding it up to the light, Doc said to himself, "Uh huh."

Not wanting to interrupt his concentration, Pa and I stood waiting for his verdict. At last, he asked Pa; "Ya got any whiskey 'round here, Harry?"

I was pretty sure he did, as I had ran across a bottle now and then when cleaning out the box stall mangers and some times bringing a quart to the surface when scooping out some oats from the bin for the chickens.

Somewhat surprised, Pa replied, "Why, yes, I do happen to have some."

"Well, get it."

Crossing through the gangway, Pa disappeared into the other side of the barn, returning shortly with a quart bottle more than half full and handed it to Doc Dale.

Since there was gonna be another drenching of the cow, I glanced up on the wall to be sure the round-nosed plier-like tongs were on hand as we would surely need them to control that cow. She had hated the Epson Salts badly enough, but this was bound to be worse.

Holding the dark bottle up to the light to figure out the amount it contained, Doc unscrewed the cap, tipped it up and took two or three long pulls from it. As we stood in open-mouthed surprise, Doc Dale made the God-awfullest scrinched-up, and pucker-lipped expressions as the firewater did its thing. Then he sucked in several fast breaths to cool his burning throat. Getting things back under control, except for the tears in his eyes, he whispered hoarsely, "Damn, that's good!"

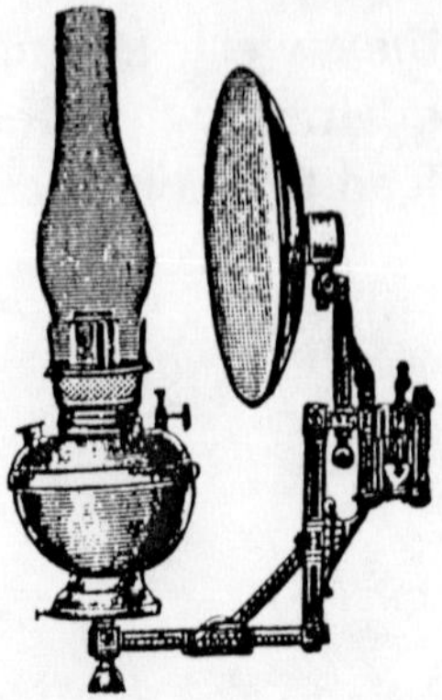

Coming out of his state of awe, Pa stated somewhat indignantly, "What the hell? I thought you were gonna give that to the cow."

Feigning surprise himself, Doc Dale stood holding the bottle by the neck as if preparing himself for another charge. With his eyebrows raised and a very noticeable twinkle in his eyes, said. "Give it to the cow? Good grief! Harry, ya been farming all these years, an' ya don't know whiskey don't do a cow no damn good, at all?"

'Sides, she's got iron in her gut an' it's punctured. She's as good as dead."

In spite of the impending loss of the animal, Pa, being far from short of a sense of humor, guffawed and snatched the bottle from Doc's hand and tipped it up for a pull himself.

Seeing there was nothing more I could do and that they were undoubtedly going to get better acquainted while the whiskey lasted, I went out to feed the horses and finish the rest of the chores.

During the years that followed, whenever we needed a vet, we'd call Doc Dale. If it was possible to bring an ailing critter back to health, Doc Dale could do it. Doc Dale had been at the game so long that, with few exceptions, he knew when he had a chance or when he didn't. No use eatin' up a small farmer in fees for a losing battle.

Another curious trait that Doc Dale had, for a veterinarian, was his dislike of dogs.

Now, if you happened to have a good-with-livestock farm dog, that was different. His main repulsion rested on what he called, "Them damned viperish little ankle-chewin' lap dogs the widows an' ol' maids keep bringin' in for me to treat, when there ain't a damn thing wrong with 'em."

I called his office one morning, explaining I had a ruptured pig. Since I had to come to town on some other errands, I ask if he'd be in his office I'd just bring the pig with me, and he could sew it up right there in his office.

"Sure, bring 'im in. I got some work to do here, so I'll be in all morning.

I tied the legs of that contrary porker and put him in the trunk of the car.

Arriving at Doc Dale's rather unkept office, he was not at his desk. I supposed he had stepped out for a minute so I sat down in a chair holding my now docile pig by his hind legs.

All of a sudden I heard a commotion comin' from the back room where he kept cages to hold those "damned viperish little ankle-chewin' lap dogs."

It sounded like cage doors bein' slammed, a dog yapping and some low unintelligible cuss words from Doc. This was all climaxed by a high pitched ky-kying from what sounded like maybe a Boston bulldog or maybe a terrier of some sort that's jus' had a boot planted in his ribs.

Just then Doc's telephone began ringing. He never had a helper or a secretary, so the phone would just have to ring 'til he got around to answering it. Evidently the caller knew this and hung right in there.

By and by Doc came through the swinging doors muttering something about a stupid mutt to himself. Noticing me, he nodded and picked up the phone. The lady on the other end talked in a loud and shrill voice, easily loud enough that I could overhear her.

That lady wanted to know if there was any improvement in her little dog, "Poopsie."

Giving me a slow wink, Doc Dale said, "Yeah, Mrs. Winkler. Yer dog's improved markedly today. In fact, I just got done giving him another "treatment", you kin pick 'em up anytime.

Coming as near to smiling as I ever saw him, he dug around in his old desk, coming up with a needle and catgut. As I held the pig upside down between my legs, he quickly repaired the rupture and I was on my way.

CHAPTER VI

HOW NOT TO CATCH A GROUNDHOG

When I was a young lad, I was an avid groundhog hunter. My favorite territory was the railroad right-of-way that ran through our little town. Its banks and fills were punctured with hog dens. Every weekend my dog, Theodore or Ted (he answered to either name), and I lay in wait for them to come out of their holes to forage. If one ventured far enough away from his den, I'd let Ted fight it to the finish. If not, I'd blow him away with my old shotgun.

Theodore was a cross between a German shepard and an Alaskan husky. The cross, in his case anyhow, matched up superior intelligence and love of battle with a thick wooly coat almost impervious to his opponent's teeth. A full-grown groundhog can put up a hell of a fight, no pushover for any dog.

The bounty on a pair of hog ears was ten cents. It was not enough for a boy to get rich on, but it kept me in candy and pop. It was a pretty good deal, even at ten cents a pair.

One day I stopped at the store to replenish my supply of candy and pop. Lyle Coffee asked me why I didn't catch him a live groundhog or two.

He said he'd give me a dollar and a half each. He wanted them alive to put in a gunny sack to drag trail for training his field trial dogs.

"A dollar and a half? I'd sure like to, Lyle, but I ain't got any traps an' they won't hold still for live catchin' anyhow."

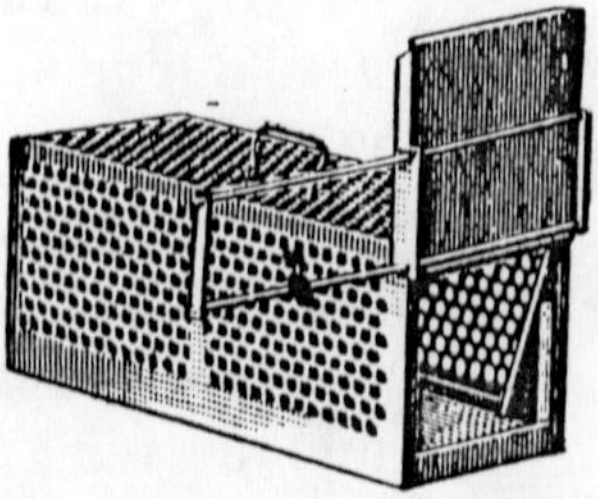

"Oh, no. I'll tell ya how to do it. Ya get a couple gallons of kerosene or gasoline, an' maybe mix the two. Get ya a gunny sack to hold over the hole. Be sure an' plug all the other holes he might have an' leave the hole open ya pour gas down an' the one ya want to put the sack over. The fire will follow the stream of fuel right down in the den an' out he'll come runnin' right in the sack!"

Well, that sounded easy as fallin' off a log. I good as had that money in my pocket.

I didn't say anything to Pa about it. I'd heard him say several times that pouring gas in his old tractor was like pouring it down a hole in the ground. I figured he wouldn't take too much to me actually doing it, when he wasn't around I took two gallons out of the fuel barrel and hid it.

I also got a neighbor buddy of mine, Jake Bewely, to agree to come along to hold the sack. I knew I wouldn't be able to light the fuel and hold that sack too. I promised Jake a share of the profits, so he was all cocked and primed to go along.

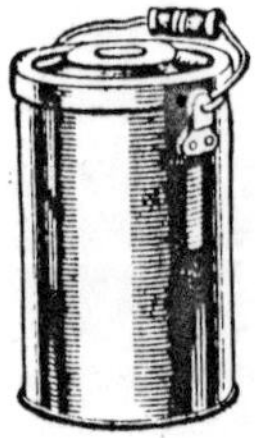

On Saturday morning Jake and I picked up the can of gas I'd hidden. I gave Ted a whistle and we trooped down the road to the tracks.

It wasn't but about five minutes until we spotted an old grinder sticking his head up out of his den. When we got too close, he ducked down into what he thought was complete safety. Ted smelled him and started digging like crazy. He was silly about that. He'd dig like all get out, throwing dirt out from between his hind legs. Every once in a while he'd back up, dragging his front paws so as to move the dirt back making room for more. He'd chew off roots that got in his way, growling and talking to himself. I think, about what he was going to do to that rascal when he got down to him. Then he'd stop digging for a minute and shove himself down in the hole up to his shoulders to snort and smell to reassure himself the hog was still in there.

Satisfied that his prey hadn't escaped him, old Ted would go at it with renewed vigor.

If it wasn't too hot, he'd stay there working for sometimes a half day; I don't know how many he'd tried to dig out, always failing.

I wondered about old Ted. You'd have thought a dog as smart as Ted was in other ways would figure out after a while that it was useless. I told him and told him it wasn't any use wasting time and work on it. I'd call him away and try to get him interested in something else. He'd leave long enough to see what I had to offer. If it didn't prove to be what my pretended excited voice claimed, he'd go back to his digging again. Ya just couldn't reason with him on this point so I just gave up.

Jake and I scouted the den for back doors. This old hog had several. We got some brush and leaves and sticks and stomped them into the entrances with some dirt. We got them all plugged except the one Ted was digging in. I tried to get him to quit so we could plug it, but he wouldn't stand for it.

"Let's go ahead and let 'im dig. That old grinder likely won't come out that hole anyhow. Even if he does, ol' Ted'll have aholt of 'im an' maybe we can get the sack over the hog before he's hurt too bad."

So, I went ahead and poured the gas down the hole. I held my match at the ready and looked at each one of my partners. Jake nodded as if he was ready. Ted's tail and rear end was pointed skyward. He made a real good plug for the remaining open hole to the den.

He was snorting and blowing the loose dirt out of his nose so he could take a smell now and then.

I struck the match and dropped it down the hole. Before you could say, "Jack Robinson," there was a ground-shaking "KER-WHOMP!!"

Dirt and clods and fire leaped out of the holes. The gunny sack went flying in the air as Jake was catapulted in a backward somersault. Ted went flying backwards out of the hole amidst a cloud of dirt, smoke, and flame.

I stood there stunned. That wasn't the way it was supposed to work. I thought it'd just burn and smoke things up, giving the grounding an idea there must be better places to be.

Jake wasn't hurt, but he sure looked queer. His eyebrows and eyelashes were gone along with the fuzz on his face. He had dirt in his nose and hair. It took him a minute to get his bearings.

When the smoke cleared, Ted had retreated to the railroad tracks. He looked real bewildered. A big old train could have come along 'bout that time,

and Ted wouldn't have noticed. His whiskers were gone and the fur around his head was singed some. He'd sneeze and cough and was working his tongue like he did when I'd give him a piece of bread with a big gob of peanut butter on it. He blinked and rubbed his eyes with his paws 'til he got the dirt worked out into little mud balls at the corners.

When Ted could see again, he sat there with his tongue lolled out the side of his mouth and looked at me. I don't know if you could really say he had an expression on his face or not. But I knew that dog, had grown up with him and he had expressions, mostly in his eyes. Right then his eyes were saying something like, "Boy, that's the most ill-tempered hotheaded groundhog I've ever had any dealings with!"

We were all glad that none of us got hurt, 'cept the grinder, he never did show. The concussion, no doubt, had killed him. If not, he'd never be the same and likely Lyle wouldn't give a dollar for him now, anyway.

We gave up catchin' any more live ones, Lyle Coffee and his hounds could go to hell as far as we cared.

Of course, I kept hunting them for sport. Ted did, too. But when he ran one into the ground, that was the end of it as far as Ted was concerned. He'd had enough of that pie.

Like I said, he was a smart dog and a quick learner. As long as he lived, I never saw him stick his head in another groundhog hole.

CHAPTER VII

WATERMELON TIME

When I was a lad of fifteen, I pestered Pa into buying me an old car to knock around in. My buddy, Jack Anderson, and I chugged around the countryside getting into all kinds of mischief in that car. I guess a boy gettin' a car doesn't let him get into any more trouble than without one, it just gives him a crack at more exciting trouble.

One hot, humid Sunday afternoon in August, we picked up another friend, Dave Bewely, and we drove around looking for something to do.

Jack mentioned how good a cold watermelon would taste. It wouldn't have had to be cold, really, just a big old juicy warm one would do.

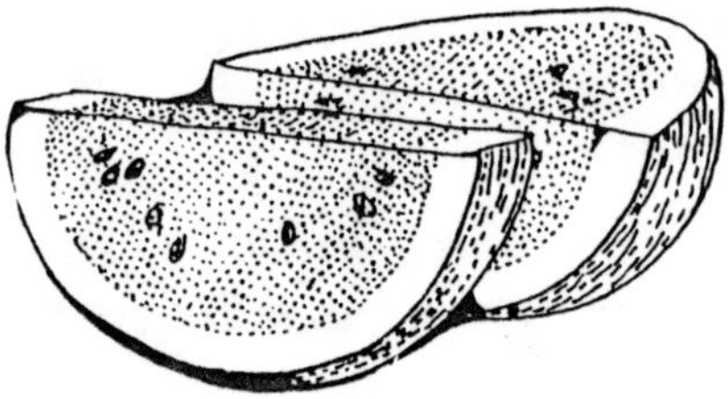

I said, "Ya know what? I think I know where we can get us a melon, maybe even four or five of 'em."

Dave and Jack leaned forward, looking at me as they asked, almost in unison, "Where?"

"I've got an old uncle, Ems Hilligoss, who raises watermelons for his roadside stand down by New Boston on the Mississippi River bottoms. Might be, if we play our cards right, we could lift a few from him."

"New Boston," Jack cried out. "That's twenty miles away. We got 'nough gas to get there an' back?"

I pulled over to the side of the road and stopped, dug my measuring stick out from under the seat, unscrewed the gas cap and took a reading. Only the bottom inch of the stick came out wet, which meant that we had only a gallon or so.

Replacing the cap, and the seat cushion, I said, "Well, guys, that ain't enough. It'll take about a dollar's worth for the trip, along with the scouting around we'll have to do to locate his field and get the lay of things. I haven't been to Uncle Ems' since I was a real little fella. I remember how to get to his farm, but there's no tellin' which field he's got the melons planted in. If it's too close to the house we got problems, 'cause I remember Pa tellin' how handy Ems is with his old shotgun."

This fact impressed Jack and Dave, but not to the point that made them want to give the project up. It just added a little spice to the venture.

We all dug down in our bib overall pockets and pooled eighty-two cents. We'd get about three and a half gallons for that, so with the gallon already in the tank, we'd have more than enough.

Dave said, "Now, I'm just as hungry for melons as you guys are, but I don't relish the thought of getting shot at. We gotta have a good plan."

Dave was always wantin' to be on the extra careful side, which of course, isn't too bad a fault; so we laid out our plan of attack on the way to New Boston.

It'd be about dusk when we got there and got the field located, so I said, "Here's what we'll do. I'll dump you guys out along the road as close as we dare to the field. You lay low in the grader ditch 'til it gets dark enough, then sneak over, snatch a few and hide 'em in the weeds along the bottom of the ditch. After I dump ya, I'll drive on to Uncle Ems' an' keep 'im busy visitin' 'til I think you've had time enough. That way you won't have to worry 'bout him lurkin' around with his shotgun.

"That sounds like a good enough plan to me," Dave agreed. Jack nodded his head with eager excitement.

I located Ems' house without any trouble and as we drove slowly by we could see him puttering around his tractor.

The melon patch was easy to spot. The big dark green humps could be seen right from the road above the solid mat of lighter colored leaves and vines. The only thing was, they weren't as far away from his house as I would have preferred.

Well, we couldn't help that. We'd made the trip clear down here and weren't going back without giving it a whirl.

I slowed down enough for Jack and Dave to jump out where they disappeared, sliding down the bank into the tall horseweeds. Driving on the eighth of a mile or so to Ems', I turned off the sandy bottom land into his driveway. He was just backing his tractor up to hook onto a hayrack mounded up with big old striped melons. I hurried over and raised the wagon tongue, lining it up with the drawbar and dropped the pin through. Thanking me, he killed the engine and sat studying me a moment.

I said, I don't imagine you remember me, Uncle Ems. I'm Mable and Harry's youngest boy."

His eyes lit up right away. "By damn! I knew you resembled someone in the family. I should have guessed it. By gad! You've growed since I last seen ya."

He asked how Mable and Harry were, then sat down on the wagon tongue and studied on how long it'd been since we last visited him. I reminded him it'd been about nine years.

"By gad! It's been that long, has it? Well, time goes by purty fast when ya get as old as I am. You likely won't notice it for a spell yet, but you will one day."

We visited along a bit, then Ems must have caught me eyeballing the rack full of watermelons and said, "You folks don't have much luck raisin' melons up there on the prairie, do ya? By gad, that's one thing this river sand will grow. Would you like to have one er two to take home with ya?"

"I sure would, Uncle Ems. But I ain't got any money. Spent the last we . . . . er, I had for gas."

"Hells' bells, boy! I wouldn't think of chargin' kinfolk for a melon er two. Just pick whatever ya want off the wagon there, an' take 'em along home."

I picked out a pair that looked the ripest, opened the truck of the car and rolled 'em in. An uneasy kind of guilty feeling was beginning to crawl up my spine. In fact, it was crawling so fast I thought it best if I got away from there as fast as decency allowed.

Not being able to look him in the eye, I thanked him for the melons while I bent over to crank up the car. It was nearly dark now. Dave and Jack had had plenty of time and might be getting nervous. As I climbed in under the wheel, Ems stepped back a bit with his hat in his hand to wave as I pulled away.

"Glad to see ya, nephew. You be sure an' tell your folks I said to come on down sometime. An' you come back again sometime, even if it ain't melon ripinin' season. But if it does happen to be, why you just come right on up to the house here an' I'll give ya some more melons."

Possibly because of my guilty feelings, I noticed a humorous smile and an extra sparkle to his eyes as he added. "An' next time ya might's well bring them other fellas up too, 'cause I'd like to meet 'em. That way they wouldn't have to pack their findin's so far."

I turned dead pale, then pink, then red. Finally I answered weakly, "Yeah . . ., okay, Uncle Ems."

As I guided the car out of the driveway, I felt so damned cheap and small that I could barely see over the hood.

I never went back to Uncle Ems' until I was a grown man and he was nearing eighty. Neither of us mentioned that time although the twinkle in his eyes told me he remembered it as well as I did. He sensed, I'm sure, how mortified I was and still am about that little caper.

CHAPTER VIII

THE PRIDE OF ANDER AND SIGNA

There's an old saying concerning the raising of children. "As the twig is bent, so grows the tree."

In the majority of cases, no doubt this is true, but what is the mysterious element or chance gene that oft-times throws this old proverb out of kilter?

I never knew Ander and Signa Anderson personally. They died before my time. However, I felt I knew them from overhearing my parents' and grandparents' conversations about them.

Ander and Signa Anderson immigrated to this country from Sweden about 1880. Young and newly married,

they spent their last Krone for passage on an old freighter to escape an impoverished and starving Sweden of that time.

They were devout followers of the Lutheran faith, never missing Sunday services or taking a meal without giving thanks to the Almighty.

On their arrival in the Midwest, they quickly found employment. Self-denying and well-schooled in ways of existing on meager, earning, they saved each penny toward the time when they might purchase some land they could work and call their own, a thing not possible in the old country.

During those early, striving years, three children were born to them without benefit of doctor or hospital.

The first, a girl they named Ruby, married quite young, and moved to California with her new husband. She was never heard from again. Her whereabouts and success or failure in life was never to be learned.

Next came a boy whose name I have forgotten. He lived but a month after birth. And, last, another boy christened Frank was born.

Ander had wanted many sons to carry on his name in the new country, but this was not to be. Signa never conceived again for reasons we'll never know.

So, Frank was the apple of his parents' eyes. Signa showered him with love as one would fully expect her to.

Ander loved him no less, but not being an outgoing sort of man, he showed his love in the only way he could. He prepared the boy for life . . . how to farm, work and to be conservative in money matters that would enable Frank to eventually take over, and hopefully add to what he and Signa would someday leave to him.

While Frank was still a baby, his parents bought and managed to pay for fifty acres of unimproved Iowa farmland. By the time they got a house, barn, and other necessary outbuildings built, fences put up, and the land cleared for the plow, Ander and Signa were pretty much "over the hill."

They were rightfully proud of their accomplishment and felt little remorse for the years of worry, toil, and bone-weary hard work they had done.

Ander was a leader in the Community Lutheran Church. On brief ocassions, he took over the reading of services when the elderly Reverend was unable to.

Frank attended special Bible classes held for the

young people in the neighborhood. On confirmation, he was presented with a new Bible and his graduation picture was framed and hung on the church vestible wall with the rest of his class. Ander and Signa were grateful and so very proud to have such a devoted, hard-working son.

Frank was not what you'd call handsome. He wasn't what you'd call ugly, either, just sort of homely. He was long of arm, leg, nose, and tooth. But he did have a pleasant disposition, kind and warm-hearted. At times it bothered his parents that the boy seemed disinterested in the opposite sex. However, that would come along in time and little doublt was held that he would someday marry and give them many grandchildren. There were several young girls of Swedish ancestry close by who would take no beauty prizes but would make the best of mothers and workmates.

At the time of his father's death, Frank was twenty-four. He now took over all the farm work which old Ander had prepared him so well to do. Not expecting to meet the grim reaper so suddenly, Ander had neglected teaching Frank about the management of money and the necessary bookkeeping skills so vital to sucessful farming.

Signa took over this part of the work and things went along well until the following year when she developed what was termed, in those days, as "female trouble." Within six months, Frank laid her to rest beside his father.

Frank was now the sole owner of the farm, livestock, machinery, and all. He was pretty young for so much work and responsibility, being alone as the was.

Now, the big house seemed too quiet. He became lonely and wanted someone to laugh with and to talk to. Having has his nose kept to the grindstone during his growin up years, he'd made few close friends. The evenings after the farm chores were done seemed to get longer and longer. He decided to cast about and see if there wasn't something to do in this world besides work.

He began, occasionally at first, making trips to Tylerville in the evening on old Hazel, his father's driving mare, to swap stories with the boys and play some cards or a few games of dominoes.

In the course of these outings, Frank fell in with what may be called, in mild terms, the wrong crowd. They acquainted him with booze, which seemed to allow his shedding some of the natural shyness and timid ways his environment had molded him to.

Being rather well-fixed financially for one so young, his new "friends" stuck close by. Frank was no longer lonely.

Because of his scrupulous upbringing, he had, quite naturally, retained innocence beyond his years and was totally unaware of the long-term affects whiskey had on some men. He did know he liked the taste of it and the fun and camaraderie the spirts brought about.

Within a period of two years, his farming ability and the interest he'd once had in the work had diminished to the point that he decided to sell out.

He sold the farm much too cheaply to a clever neighbor who deceived his young neighbor. Frank then held a public auction to dispose of what stock remained, along with the machinery and house furnishings.

Now, with his pockets well lined and his purse strings loosened with booze and friends, he found it difficult to manage his newfound freedom. It seemed wherever he went, he was more than welcome.

The Andersons had never owned an automobile or tractor either, for that matter. Horse power had always done their field work. Once a week, on Saturday, old Ander had hitched Hazel to the cart and drove the family to a country general store two miles distant to do their trading.

Now, young Frank decided he needed a car. There were doubts, really, as to this being his own idea . . . or the suggestion from one of his friends. No matter, he needed transportation of a more modern sort than the aging Hazel could furnish.

A three or four hundred dollar Ford or Chevrolet would have been sufficient and had Frank been sober the day he decided to make the purchase, there is little doubt but what he would have chosen this common sort of car. But, no, he decided a better than average auto-mo-bile as he pronounced it, would be better.

He still had a thousand dollars left from the sale of the farm, a huge sum for 1931 with the Depression in full swing. He carried it stuffed in the top front pocket of his bib overalls with the snap securely fastened.

The day he decided to make the purchase, he was with Jack Raferty, a nearby neighbor of good character who liked to imbibe on occasion. The two of them had caught a ride to town and had spent most of the day drinking together at the taverns on Boone's Avenue. During a lull in their merrymaking, Frank looked out the front windows at the lengthening shadows and declared, "Jack, by gosh, we'd best be lookin' into a ride home."

Home, to Frank, was with a bachelor friend he'd moved in with after selling his place. Hilmer Rising had been more than glad to share his two-room shanty with Frank. With him living there, Hilmer didn't have to beg a can of sardines or maybe a wedge of longhorn cheese from the country grocery to get him by until he might earn a few

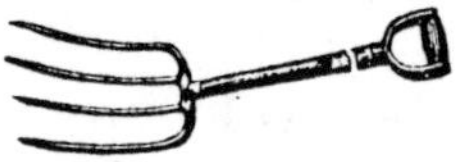

dollars haying or hauling manure for a neighbor. Frank always paid cash for their eats and it was seldom when they didn't have plenty to drink. This was more than enough to suit Hilmer. He'd never seriously thought of charging Frank rent.

Jack sat a minute trying to get his eyes focused out the window to see if he agreed that it was about time to leave. Unable to determine much, he nodded, taking Frank's word for it.

"By damn, Jack, I'm tired a lookin' an' askin' for a ride home with someone an' sometimes havin' to walk. Let's drink up an' go down the street here aways. There's an out-erfit there sells auto-mobiles. Mebee we kin ride home in style."

The dealer he chose was for the LaSalle, a big, costly prestigous line. The quick-eyed salesman, spotting them walk in the drive, quickly judged he might have a pidgeon on the hook. Their unsteady gait and manner of dress being somewhat disheveled, belied either of them having much money, but the shifty clerk had long ago learned you couldn't judge the wealth of these farmers by their dress.

A glistening, new '31 LaSalle sedan stood in front of the windows of the showroom floor. Frank and Jack walked slowly around it, hands in their bib overall pockets.

"You fellows interested in buying a car today?"

"Might be," Frank drawled.

The salesman lit into his carefully prepared and reheared sales pitch on the merits, quality of workmanship and ease of operation, etc., of the car. Had he known the full degree of pidgeon he had hooked, he could have saved himself all the effort of that.

Not wishing to interrupt his long tirade, Frank stood as if listening and carefully weighing each boast and claim. He understood little or nothing about this feature or that. When the fellow finally came up for air, Frank asked, "How much is it?"

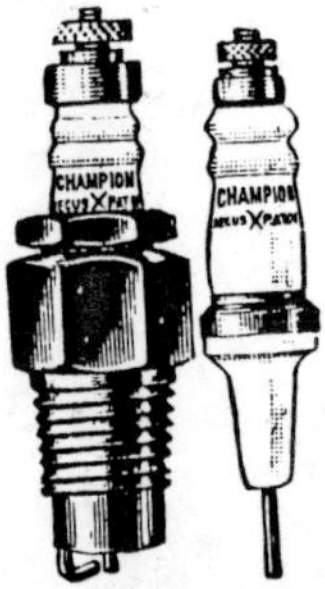

"Now there you've hit the crux of the thing! This is the last one of this model we have. Can't keep enough of 'em on hand, seems like. I'm sure the boss will agree that we should sacrifice this last car at a special low price. You're lucky you stopped in today, 'cause tomorrow at this price we've marked this beauty down to, it will be snapped up quick!! -Uh, how much did you figure on paying for a car?"

"Waal," Frank studied the floor with his bloodshot eyes, "Not over a thousand dollars."

Nearly swallowing the gum he'd been chewing and snapping, the salesman's jaw dropped open before he could stop it. Trying to cover his wits, he shook his head wonderingly.

"Well now, if that isn't something! I've been selling automobiles for many years and this is the first time I can remember this happening! Would you believe, Mr. . . . . .?"

"Frank Anderson."

"Would you believe, Mr. Anderson, the price of this beautiful automobile is nine hundred, ninety-five dollars? With the servicing done and the gas tank filled, a thousand dollars will have you breezing down the road in the grandest of style!"

Unfastening the snap of his bib pocket, Frank withdrew a wad of bills and began counting out the fifty and hundred dollar bills into the salesman's palm.

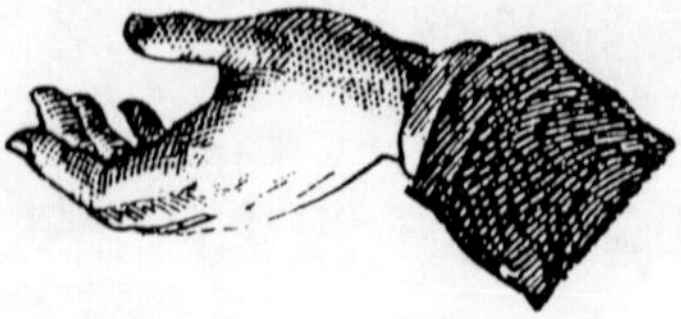

Swallowing hard, the salesman coughed once, too late. The gum was down too far to retrieve.

When the car was finally serviced, filled with gas and backed out of the garage, the salesman stood holding the door for Frank to climb in.

"You should be very proud to own such a fine car, Mr. Anderson. Take good care of it and it will give you find dependable service for many years."

Jack stood back waiting for Frank to motion him to get in. He wasn't sure if everything was done. With all the hustle and bustle, he'd stood off a ways so as not to get run over or into. Some of the booze he'd drank had wore off a bit as he waited and watched in awe of having seen someone spend more money, so quickly, than he'd thought possible.

Frank climbed in under the wheel, and sat staring at the levers, pedeals, dials, and doodads.

"How do ya git it to go?"

"How do you . . . . ! Good heavens!, Mr. Anderson, haven't you ever driven car before?"

"Nope."

"Well . . . ., how 'bout your friend over there? Can he drive?"

"Jack? Naw, don't think so. 'Sides, he just wants a ride home. Anyways, he wants to learn to drive, he'll have tuh git a auto-mo-bile of his own."

"Oh, well . . . ., if that's the case, maybe I'd better ride around the block a time or two with you to acquaint you with the operation and the shifting of gears.

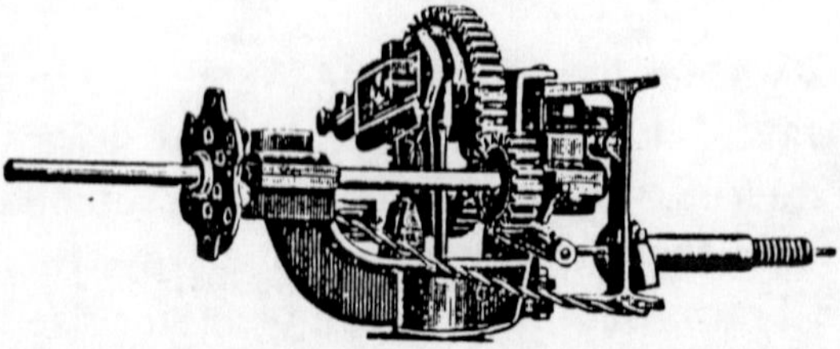

Getting in the other side, he instructed Frank how to start the engine, press down on the clutch to allow the shifting lever to be placed in low gear. Releasing the clutch pedal unevenly they lurched out into the street narrowly missing a light pole and causing an oncoming car to veer sharply up over the curbing to avoid a collision, ending up in the used car lot astraddle a sign advertising "Kendall . . . the two thousand mile oil."

This sudden happening caused Frank to tighten his grip on the steering wheel and to stiffen his legs which made the foot feed even more depressed.

About this time the salesman really became excited.

"Slow down!! Look out!! The clutch . . . . . shove in the clutch!!"

Frank was far too busy trying to stay between the sidewalks. Each time he turned away, he oversteered, making the big car careen sharply, throwing the passenger first one way, then the other. Frank was taken by complete surprise at the power and ease of turning the wheel from full right to full left and couldn't seem to ease up enough to bring the thing under control. The nearest thing he'd ever drove before like that was a pair of runaway horses.

He even tried his habitual command to them.

"Whoa, whoa!!!"

This, of course, didn't help in the least. If anything, it seemed to incite the big straight eight motor to a higher pitch.

As they approached an intersection, the salesman caught just glances of the coming danger as he was pitched to and fro. Timing his being thrown against the door for the fourth or fifth swerve, he grabbed the door handle, allowing himself to be pitched out head over heels where he rolled up against the curbing.

Watching in horror, the salesman saw Frank roar toward a railroad crossing with a train coming along at a real good clip.

Miraculously Frank swerved, missing the train and sped on his way out of town, completely unaware of what had almost happened. He was also unaware that in all the excitement two Model T cars had collided in an effort to escape him. Those Model T's were back there spouting steam and water from their burst radiators. Within that cloud of steam, parts methodically began to fall off those two innocent T's. Miscellaneous parts and pieces fell onto the brick paving, making clinks" and "clanks", each differing in sound, depending on the weight and makeup of the part.

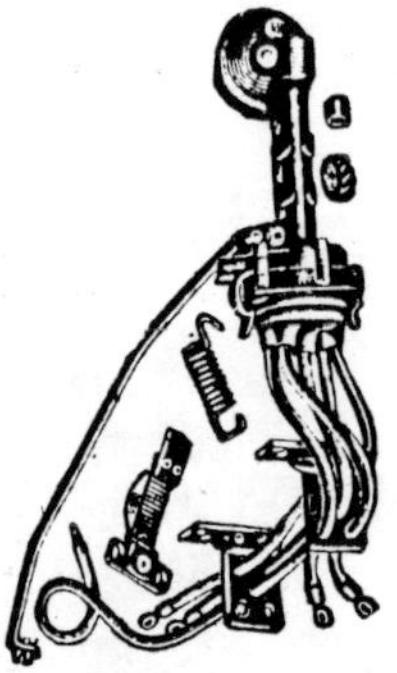

The rumblings of boiling water, hissing steam, and the sound of clattering pieces of headlights and other parts being dropped were all climaxed by two shotgun-like blasts as injured front tires of the high-pressure type blew out, allowing the wrecks to settle down somewhat.

Meanwhile, Frank was pretty busy. The straight eight was still in low gear and roaring like a giant Rumely oil pull tractor. The noise was beginning to grate on Frank's nerves somewhat and his head was beginning to ache from the day's drinking. He wished he had time to reach in his back pocket for the pint bottle of whiskey he'd bought before leaving the tavern.

His driving was improving somewhat. The wild careening from one side of the street to the other had tapered off as he began getting the hang of the thing. He muttered to himself as he attempted to reach in his rear pocket, "Gol' damned salesman. Lotta help he was, no longer'n he stayed with me. He might's well stayed where he was. Be damaned if'n I'd throwed myself out like that. Man could get hurt."

Frank managed to extract the bottle from his pocket, pull the cork out with his teeth, and tip his head back for a swallow. All this took his eyes off the road right at a most inopportune moment. The LaSalle gave a hard bounce as it dropped off the brick paving onto the rough, poorly maintained gravel road. Frank jerked the wheel, while his foot rose up and down on the accelerator with the bouncing of the car. The mouth of the bottle struck Frank's teeth.

"Gol' dammint, anyhow!!" he hollered out loud.

Dropping the whiskey bottle on the cushion beside him, he gave his undivided attention to what was going on outside the windshield there. This was hard to do, as the sound of liquor gurgling out of the bottle fought to distract him. The bottle was lying slightly tilted so all the elixer didn't escape, but Frank hated like all get out to see any wasted. The sight of old Ander came to him. He would not stand for any kind of waste. Everything had to be saved and used.

"Well, by damn," Frank thought. "I ain't got time to reach an' try to save that right now."

Before he could retain some kind of control, the car ran off the road, down into and across a rather wide, but shallow ditch.

The soft, grassy turf pulled the wheels in the opposite direction Frank wanted to go. He made some pretty intimiate contact with Harold Hawkinson's new, tightly stretched woven wire fence that divided his corn field from the county road.

Angry screeching and twanging of wire erupted along the right side, scraping the immaculate finish to shreds and ripping the front fender loose, bending it up into the air.

Frank cranked the steering wheel back toward the road, but the hedge fence posts disappearing down under the front kind of kept him from steering the car right.

Frank was talking out loud to himself now.

"I'll be gol' damned if this ain' the hammer headedest thing I ever got a holt of of! Ol' Harold's gonna be right put out 'bout that fence.

Finally overcoming the shock and the pull of all those things under the car, Frank got 'er back on the road but now was dragging fifty feet of wire and four fence posts.

The next hurdle was coming up fast, the turnoff from the main gravel road onto the "Irish Lane", the hardpacked dirt road to the little community of Tylerville and home. Frank knew a way had to be found to slow that car down some to make the turn, but how to do it? For some reason, he never once thought to take his foot off the foot feed. Glancing down at the foot pedals he discovered one he hadn't known about. He had no way of knowing it was a brake pedal and could be used to stop the car. With his left foot he pushed on that just to see what would happen. The big motor began laboring heavily and the car slowed down.

"Uh huh. I'm gittin' ya broke tuh harness now, ain' I? Time 'er two runnin' through fences an' the like usually tames things down some."

At this particular time, Hank Smith was walking along the Irish Lane toward town when he heard, then saw, the apparition skid around the corner on two wheels, spewing a cloud of loose gravel, dust and debris in its wake. As the car zigzagged from one side to the other, ol' Hank got real concerned as to which side of the road he should stay on to be out of the way. Trying to judge the car was bad enough without having to bother about whatever it was dragging behind, whipping back and forth down into the ditches like a giant whip.

Hank was well known for his slowness of foot and his inability to make quick decisions. But this was a special situtation, and he decided right quick what to do. Pausing only momentarily, he jumped across the ditch, vaulted over the fence, and took refuge behind the barrier offered by that split-rail fence.

Frank was once again gaining some kind of control, swerving away short of going into the ditches. The wire and fence posts he was dragging cut a much wider arc, destroying roadside signs and anything else it came in contact with. Coming abreast of where Hank crouched behind the rails, the crack-the-whip action threw the heavy hedge posts that were still securely stapled to the wire against an upright oak post bracing the fence. It jerked that brace loose, causing several sections to fall domino-like.

Though his oak fortress was destroyed, Hank stood untouched in open-mouthed wonder as the conglomeration roared on, disappearing quickly in a cloud of red dust.

Picking his way carefully over the hodgepodge of broken and scattered rails, Hank shook his head, saying to himself, "I'll be doggone if it's safe to be out on the roads anymore. If I ain't lost my sight all the way, that was Frank Anderson drivin' that car!"

Regaining the road, he stood a few seconds watching the fading dust cloud. "Naw, it couldn't abeen. Frank can't drive a car."

In the meantime, Frank had decided to stop at Bernard Milan's place, that is if he could get stopped.

Bernard lived about a half mile this side of Hilmar Rising's. He drove an old car himself. That is, he did when it'd run or when he could scrape up fifty cents or a dollar for gas. Bernard knew how to drive a car, so Frank figured he could show him something about the running of his new LaSalle. Besides, he wanted to show it off some. He was getting close to home and hadn't got to show it to anyone 'cept ol' Hank who hadn't even bothered to wave.

Nearing Bernard's place, he crammed the brake pedal. That's what had slowed him before so he was more sure this time.

The front end of the LaSalle dipped down as the front wheels locked up jerking Frank's prominent nose down on the steering wheel. His foot slipped off the pedal, and he was then slammed back against the cushion again.

"I'll be gol' damned if this ain' the wildest most cantankerous thing! Go like all get out, then plant its feet like it's stepped on a bridle rein."

Pressing the brake again, more carefully this time, he overpowered the straining engine, jerking to a stop, and killing the motor a few yards beyond Bernard's mailbox.

Steam boiled up around the radiator cap and hissed out around the long wire-scarred hood. Bernard stood with his hands in his pockets at the edge of his yard, trying to figure out what was going on.

Bernard and Maxine, his wife, and their six kids lived from hand to mouth by his working a few days a week on the WPA. They were what was known as "shanty Irish" and Bernard was well known by the observant to be a rather ornery individual.

Frank sat, still gripping the steering wheel, hardly believing he'd finally brought things to a halt.

Bernard, quite surprised, hailed him. Where did you get that car, Frank?"

"Jus' bought 'er in town. Damn tired of walkin' where I wanted to go. She's a beauty, ain' she?"

Bernard stepped across the ditch and walked slowly around the big car, stepping carefully over the tangle of woven wire caught up under the rear springs somehwere.

"Yeah, I kin see it was. What happened to this side over here, Frank? Looks a little worse for wear. Where'd ya gather up the wire and posts at?"

"That b'longs tuh Harold Hawkinson. I hit some mean bumps an' lost the road a minute an' run along his field awhile 'til I could git back, an' kinda tangled up his wire some. I figure Harold's gonna be put out 'bout that fence."

"Ya just come from town, huh? Bring anything to drink with ya?"

Frank picked up the bottle from the wet cushion and held it up to the light. "Got 'bout two or three swallers left. Spilt most of it while I was in Harold's fence. You're sure'n welcome to it if ya want it, Bernard."

As Bernard took the bottle from him, Frank continued, "It ain't much, but Jack, he's got a bot . . ., oh, oh, Jack's still in town standin' at the auto-mo-bile sellin' place. He wanted to ride home with me an' I plumb forgot! Bet he's madder'n all get out, having tuh walk all the way when he knowed I was comin' right closet tuh his place."

Bernard tipped the bottle up, draining the last drop. Through gritting teeth as the whiskey burned its way down, he asked, "how much this machine cost you, Frank?"

"Thousand dollars!" Frank answered proudly.

Bernard gave a long, low whistle.

"What gear'd ya have it in to make it boil and smoke the way it does? Acts like it's been in some kinda race, or somethin'".

"Gear?" Frank puzzled. "I don't know nuttin' 'bout gears. I jus' done like the salesman tol' me to do when we . . ., I left town.

He said he was gonna show me how to do this 'n that, an' b'fore you could say "scat" he ups an' jumps out, not tellin' me much of anything."

Bernard leaned in the window, glancing at the gear shift.

"Good grief! You drove all the way out here in low gear? No wonder it sounded like a road grader comin'."

"I 'spose so, but I'll tell ya, Bernard, the reason I stopped by was to have ya show me how tuh run the thing proper. You know how to drive. I gotta hit back for town an' git Jack. By damn! I bet he's just a chompin' an a fonchin' 'cause I run off an' left him thata'way."

Bernard eyed the car over, a chuckle or two escaping in spite of himself.

"Might be. But from the looks of things, he might be happier he's walkin."

"Well, I'll tell ya, Frank, I can't go back to town with ya to pick up Jack. I gotta stay here tuh the house, but I'll help ya all I kin to get ya started right. Likely that's what caused all your problems, not gettin' started out right."

"Now then, put your foot on the clutch pedal there an' push it to the floor. Hold 'er down now an' start the motor."

Frank did as directed. The straight eight had cooled enough to allow an easy start, though some grinding noises come from under the hood that made Bernard grit his teeth.

"Now, you've already got it in first gear, so jus' press down hard on that foot feed pedal there to the right an' hold it to the floor. When she gits to a high pitch an' sounds like the power is up, just jerk yer foot off that clutch pedar there, an' you're on your way."

Frank did as directed again. But as the roar and pitch of the big eight increased, he wasn't just sure when it was right. Bernard had retreated back across the ditch to be at a safe distance. Frank glanced at him wondering if things were ready and looking for a sign. Bernard nodded his head and Frank gave his undivided attention to gripping the steering wheel, ready to watch the road ahead. Then he dropped the clutch.

For a split second the LaSalle seemed suspended in midair as it ripped and tore for traction. Had Frank been sober, there's little doubt but what the first lunge would have given him a bad case of whiplash. The big sedan came down to terra firma, found substantial traction, gave another violent lurch and self-destructed on the spot . . . . clutch and pressure plate, along with pieces of cast aluminum transmission housing (with a gear or two still attached) spinning like crazy amid a shower of hot smoking oil.

The right rear axle snapped just before the drive shaft broke loose and came spinning crookedly from underneath, finishing its whirling in the grader ditch.

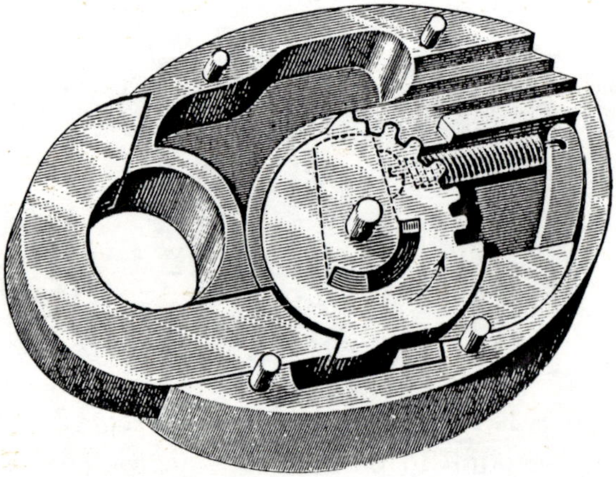

Frank held onto the steering for dear life, like he figured all this commotion was just preliminary to getting under way. Silence, however, once again fell over the quiet neighborhood when the straight eight locked up amid a cloud of smoke and steam.

Bernard fell to the ground in a helpless fit of glee, rolling over and over on the ground.

Frank slowly dismounted and stood with his hands in his pockets, surveying the smoking ruins, glancing at Bernard occasionally as if wondering what in the world could have tickled him so.

"What the matter with you, Bernard?"

All Bernard could do was to kind of raise and wave one hand and then resume his laughter.

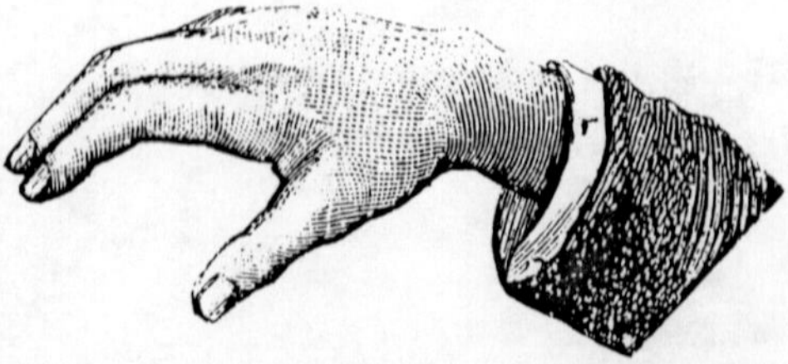

Heaving a sigh, Frank began walking down the road toward Hilmer's place. He'd glance back over his shoulder every few steps to see if Bernard had maybe raised up. He talked out loud to himself as he continued on.

"Gol damned auto-mo-bile likely never was any good. Prob'ly why I got it so cheap. Gol damned salesman wuz a shyster, I betcha. I ever run into him agin, I'm gonna see if he kin talk so good with my thumbs on his Adam's apple."

Climbing the steep roadside bank in front of Hilmer's house, he saw his buddy get up out of his broken rocking chair and step down off the rickety front porch. Hilmer had spotted Frank coming up the road. He knew he'd likely been to town and had brought a bottle with him. Hilmer was dry, very dry.

He was tickled no end to see Frank coming home this early in the evening with something to drink.

"Ho! By yee! Frank, ya been to town, have ya?"

"Yeah, jus' came from there."

"By yee, ya bring a bottle witcha, did ya? Shore could use a swaller 'er two."

"Well, yeah, I had one, but same of it split out and Bernard drank the rest."

"Bernart? By yee, whatcha wanta stop at Bernart's fer?"

"I stopped to see if he'd show me how to drive my new auto-mo-bile, but he didn't know any more 'bout it than that damn salesman did."

"New car?" Where you got a new car at? I been settin' here on my front porch most the afternoon. I ain' seed no car go by."

Hilmer looked up and down the road again, now, to make sure he hadn't missed anything.

"It's down at Bernard's. He was trying' to show me how to drive it when it broke down."

"Dammit, Frank, I can't figure why ya wanta give Bernart a drink for. He's always wantin' a drink, but he ain' got notten of his own."

Hilmer was disgusted to the point of anger. He hadn't had a drink for two days. He'd been asked by a neighbor to help with his haying, but it being so hot, he'd decided against it. Besides, having such a free-spending boarder staying with him furnishing the grub and booze, it didn't seem necessary to sweat on the end of a pitchfork.

"By yee, Ed Penders is goin' to town purty soon. We'll watch for him to come out of his lane there, an' you kin give 'im two three dollars to bring us back sompin' to drink. By yee, we gotta have sompin' to drink 'round here!"

Frank wiped his long nose on his sleeve.

"Yeah, 'spect we could. But I ain't got no money."

Hilmer looked at Frank with shock and disbelief.

"Watcha mean, ya ain't got no money? You got plenty money from sellin' yer place."

Hilmer spat snuff juice on the ground with finality and looked toward the end of the rutted lane where Ed Penders would come out on his way to town. He didn't want to miss him and have him get by before they could flag him down.

"Uh huh. But the auto-mo-bile cost purty near uh thousand dollars, an' by the time I got some gas put in it, that took 'er all."

Hilmer was almost beside himself, bordering on becoming hysterical. Tobacco juice was leaking out of his mouth as his voice rose in pitch.

"You spent it all on a damn fool car? An' ya didn't bring notten home tuh drink?! By yee, Frank, you're a damn fool! We ain' got notten 'round here, an' you ain' got no money?"

"I been lettin' you stay in my house. You ain' paid no rent like ya shoulda! By, yee, ya ain' stayin' in my house no more!! You kin go!"

Frank had become used to Hilmer's noisy outbursts and wasn't much disturbed, himself not being an easily disturbed type. But he sensed that Hilmer meant it this time, so he sauntered unconcerned-like around to the back door, the only door that would open and close half-way decent on the old dilapidated shack. He gathered up his extra shirt and pair of overalls hanging over the back of the chair and dug round under the old cot he had slept on for the pair of dirty socks.

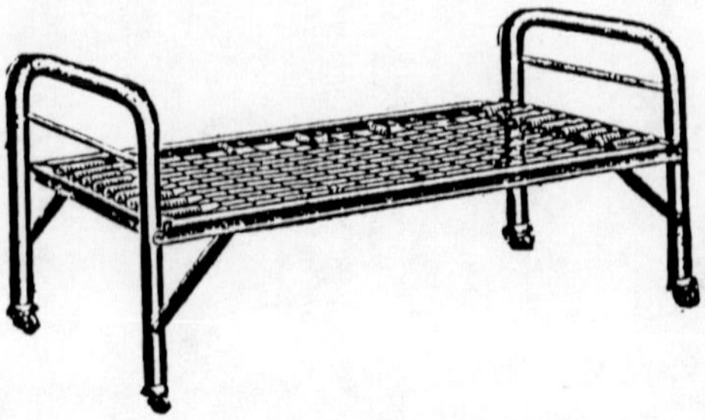

Tying his socks and stuff in a bundle he descended the bank to the road, not saying anything to Hilmer who stood watching him leave in silent contempt.

A few days later Frank sold the LaSalle for a hundred dollars, and moved away from our immediate community to a place named "Pucker Brush." It wasn't a village, but rather an area of rough and broken land, covered with buck brush and red haw. There he dug himself a cave back in the side of a steep bank, covered it over with old boards, limbs, and tarpaper. There he took up residence.

So there lived, until the day he died, Frank Anderson, the only offspring of Ander and Signa, the boy who was left to beget and continue future generations of the name.

CHAPTER IX

HE BEARS WATCHIN'

One day during my middle "teen" years, a time when I was full of vim and vigor with no sense to harness it with, Pa decided a new fence was needed across one end of our pasture.

We set the corner and brace posts and stretched a single barb wire from one end to the other at ground level to give us a straight line to dig the post holes to.

The distance across the pasture was about sixty rods and it'd take a good many holes.

Pa told me what I needed to do.

"Will, you take the spade and every three long steps you stop and tip a chunk of sod outta the ground to mark where the holes are gonna be. While you're doin' that, I'll go over to Dale

Parkinson's and see if I can borrow his tractor-mounted posthole digger. I'll be back as soon as I can."

It didn't take me long to mark out the holes. Pa wasn't back yet, so I took up the hand auger and started digging the holes three foot deep, a depth

sufficient for line posts. It was the spring of the year and good digging, so I set to my work with that vim and vigor I told about earlier.

By mid-afternoon, it was obvious the tractor auger wasn't going to be needed. I only had about another hour's diggin' left.

I finished the last hole, wiped the sweat from my brow, leaned the hand auger against the corner post and cut across the pasture towards home.

Evidently, Pa had run into trouble in borrowing the tractor outfit; possibly Dale was using it himself.

As I trudged across the pasture, I could jus see how surprised Pa was going to be when he learned I had dug them all by hand, and we needn't have waited for Parkinson's outfit. He would, no doubt, praise me and shake his head in wonder. Maybe he'd even give me an extra dollar or two when I asked.

Climbing over the gate by the driveway, I noticed our wagon standing there with no auger in it. As I had suspected, he'd been unable to borrow it. But, why hadn't he stopped on the way back and told me?

I went in the house and found Pa sitting in the living room reading the newspaper.

"You couldn't get the posthole digger, heh?"

He looked at me over the top of the paper and said, "No, I didn't get it."

In a sort of off-handed, unconcerned way, I stated, "Well, it doesn't make any difference now. We won't need it. I got 'em all dug by hand."

I waited for him to lower the newspaper and to stare at me in unbelieving wonder; but he kept on reading.

"Yeah, I figured you would, so I never bothered to go see about it."

I tried to watch him a little closer after that.

CHAPTER X

ALVIN JUNK

It was in the late fall of '44, wood-sawing time. We used a buzz saw, belt-driven by an old 10-20 McCormick Deering tractor.

The saw was staked down, the teeth sharpened, and the tractor and belt lined up. All we needed was enough help to carry the long lengths of wood to the saw. Pa and I went over to Alvin Junk's to see if he could help.

Alvin was in his late sixties, rather tall and lanky with long arms and hands that were almost massive. His features were coarse, with a few tobacco-stained snag teeth hanging in front. Alvin was nearly stone deaf. To make him hear, you had to get right up close and shout.

When we pulled up in front of his house, we could see something was going on in the shed. Blue smoke was pouring out of the doorway, along with a god-awful banging and roaring.

Alvin was tuning up his old Fordson tractor, one of Henry's first attempts to retire the horse. He had the throttle wide open. I don't know what kept it from throwing pistons and bearings out through the side of the motor. Pa stepped up beside him, touching him on the arm and hollered, "How's she runnin', Alvin?"

Alvin tilted his head back, his eyes almost closed as was his custom when he was about to say something he considered to be fact.

"Just like a sewin' machine, Harry. Purrin' like a kitten."

Alvin agreed to help after dinner. Pa said that would be fine and we let him get back to his "tuning."

After dinner, the sawing got underway. We finished one wood pile and reset the saw closer to the

next one. Charlie Pearson, the sawyer, got out his file to sharpen the saw teeth. This interval afforded us some visiting time; we were in no hurry. A rest from lifting the heavy wood was welcomed.

Restin' time between sawin' was always the time for stories, of course.

Alvin wasn't too talkative, but when he did want to say something he usually got the floor. If he didn't happen to be looking right at you, he didn't know if anyone else was talking or not. So, it didn't surprise us much when he took right off talking in the middle of something Charlie was saying.

"We always milked quite a few cows when we wuz farmin'. I'll never forgit one Saturday, me an' the folks went to town to do our tradin'. I bought me a pair of striped bib overalls. Osh-Kosh-B-Gosh was the kind they wuz. Cost quite a little, but tough an' wear like iron. I was always kinda slim and tall, so ta git a pair that was long enough, I had ta buy a pair too big around. I guess they figured if a man grew so tall he had to be big 'round, too.

Well, we stayed in town a little longer than usual, so when we got home I didn't take time to change inta my ol' clothes. It wuz gittin' late an' I didn' relish stumblin' 'round in the dark. I got the cows in an' fed 'em. Took up my milk stool an' bucket ready ta milk.

We had this old cow we called 'The Brindle'. She was a purty good cow 'cept fer some damn reason or other she'd kick ya. She only done it 'bout once a month like. 'bout the time yer bruises had gone away an' ya'd fergot the last whompin' ya got an' ya thought ever'thin' was fine, she was a cockin' and a primin' ta correct yer memory."

We all kind of shifted there where we were settin',

knowin' full well we were gonna hear about that brindle cow, if we liked it or not.

"Well, I had my stool an' bucket an' I starts to set down ta her. When I bent over, them new overalls bagged down in front where my belly was s'pposed ta be. Right then that damn cow saw her chance. She kicked, but the overalls throwed her aim off an' instead of whompin' me in the belly like she wanted, her foot went between me an' the bib on them new Osh-Kosh-B-Gosh's. It went through alright, but when she went to draw it back, fer 'nother try it was kinda like tryin' ta take a fish hook out, it got hung up, you know. She didn't think too much a havin' her leg hung up like that an' I didn't think too much of it m'self. She right away wants her foot back on the floor. I figured that'd be what she'd want

an' I tried ta undo the snaps on them suspenders.

"I guess I tried ta hurry too much 'cause I fumbled an' she got awful impatient.

"Well, Old Brindle throwed me to an' fro a couple good times, then stopped ta see what the holdup was.

" 'Bout this time I was feelin' like one of them boxin' match fellows, the one that's layin' on the floor, you know.

"I managed to pull my wits together enough ta talk to Old Brindle. I talked ta her real nice, trying' to calm her an' at the same time, trying' ta git a suspender undone.

"It wasn't a bit easy ta do all that since she had quite a bit of tension on 'em an' wouldn' give me any slack.

"I jus' 'bout had one unfastened when she decided to give it 'nother try on her own.

"Than damn cow got me down there in all the grit

and grime, kinda head first. She had me down in that stuff, kinda head first, and jus' more'n wallerin' me around in it.

"The one thing I got to wishin' and that was that I'd bought me a cheaper pair of overalls."

CHAPTER XI

A CURE FOR THE COMMON COLD

I recently contacted one of the worst colds I've ever had. It started with a slight scratchiness in my throat which seemed to have improved as the hours passed. By bedtime I was in pretty good shape again. This, of course, was a diversionary tactic. By morning I woke to find my head stopped up completely.

It was obvious that this one was going to be a real dinger. I swallowed a couple of asprin and sat down at the kitchen table holding my head and rummaging around in my memory for medicines and methods I'd used or heard of in the past.

My wife was making out her weekly shopping list and asked me if there were any medications I wanted her to pick up while she was in town. I jokingly told her a fifth of whiskey would be all right.

This spur of the moment request was triggered by my sudden remembrance of a remedy my grandfather swore by. His recipe involved whiskey, honey, and ginger.

As I sat there, staring miserably out the kitchen window at the snowdrifts, I recalled the time I had decided to put Grandpa's cure to the test. He had long since passed on, leaving no written directions as to amounts or blending. However, I figured this was of small matter since I knew the ingredients, a little experimenting should, at the very least, affect a partial cure, for he had expounded it as a complete medicine.

I had poured a tumbler half full of one hundred proof I.W. Harper straight whiskey, added four tablespoons of honey and a couple of knocks of ginger. I held it up to the light, stirring it, making sure it was mixed well. I took a mouthful and swallowed quickly to get my inner machinery set up for the shock of the remaining half pint.

Two more gasping "goes" at it and I had it down. I remember having to hold onto the table for support, struggling for my breath, and finally got it back. I wiped the tears from my eyes and went to bed.

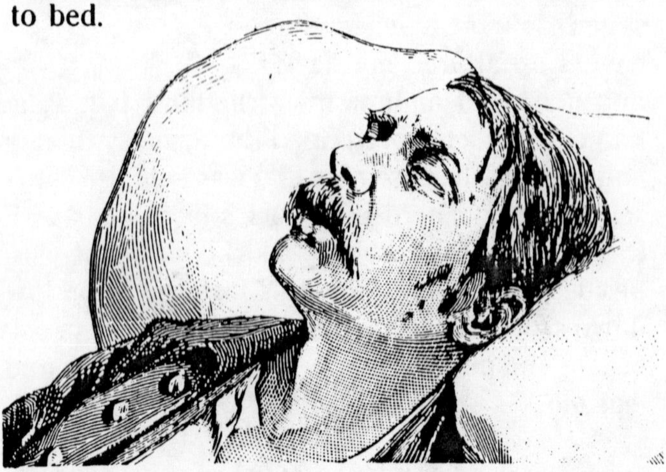

Grandpa had said to just cover up good and lie there and sweat. I lay there, halfway looking at the ceiling.

Presently, I noticed a marked improvement. I was surprised as I had had little faith in the old remedy to start with. But its medicinal qualities were making an impression on me that increased by the minute. I'd felt absolutely terrible a short while earlier. The speed with which I had recovered was extraordinary. I lay there mulling it all over.

I'd been to my doctor. He had said to get plenty

of rest, drink lots of juices, and he gave me a prescription to have filled at the drugstore. I'd looked at his scribbling on the way to Rexalls. Russian KGB agents would have been sorely tried in figuring out the code.

They gave me a little box of mean-looking orange pills that tasted like gall and cost seven dollars. I pulled the covers up around my neck and marveled at how much better I felt. Why hadn't the doctor prescribed the whiskey, honey and ginger? The answer to that was easy. He didn't sell whiskey! The damn quack's in cahoots with the druggists. Probably gets a kickback on the pills, besides two more office calls from me. The low down crooks! I always suspected they were in collusion, and now I was sure of it. Well, I had found 'em out.

Not only had I found out about how that doctor had been takin' me to the cleaners, but it was crystal clear that Grandpa's remedy was accomplishing all kinds of good stuff. I could just more'n feel those cold germs makin' tracks to get away from that concoction of whiskey, honey and ginger. Here I was a living proof of the wonders of that early remedy vs. the obvious lack of benefit of those mean-looking little orange pills the doctor had prescribed for me.

I remember deciding that I needed to spread the word about Grandpa's remedy so that other folks could have the benefits of his whiskey, honey, and ginger wonder cure.

I also decided, as I lay there, that there was no point in wasting any time on getting that done, either.

The first to know should be my friends, of course. I rose from bed forthwith, got dressed, and started out the door when the bottle of I.W. Harper caught my eye. I grabbed it up. It wouldn't hurt to have a little "proof of the pudding" to brace my statements with.

I proclaimed my discovery to my closest friends and later to some not-so-close friends. Still later I told some total strangers about it. All these folks seemed really intrigued, listening with undivided attention.

By and by my prescription ran out, and their interest flagged. My own zeal had tapered off a bit and unnoticed by me, it had gotten dark. But, no matter, I had planted the seed and it would grow.

I returned home and prepared for bed. I hadn't given the sweat part of the treatment enough opportunity to do its magic, and I knew I had to do that.

I mixed up some honey and ginger but after a

swallow I decided it lacked body and would not stand alone. I went to bed, but awoke again at the ungodly hour of three in the morning.

I sat on the edge of the bed sweating. That gratified me until I discovered it was a cold sweat, and not a very healthful one.

My cold had regressed. As I stumbled downstairs, I cursed myself for not taking the honey and ginger with me on my crusade. I chugged down some bromo, tossed in a couple of asprins for good measure, and returned to bed.

So, here I was, having recalled the details of the day I chose to try Grandpa's remedy and all the ramifications of that act. And, here I had, another cold and the opportunity to once again pay tribute to grandpa's memory or to respond to my wife's question about if there was any medication I'd want her to pick up while she was in town.

Maybe I should give that old cure another go at it. This time, if I did that, I should keep all the ingredients close at hand, of course.

But, no . . . I've done enough. These experiments should be left to younger people. They can better withstand the rigors of possible setbacks and overcome any obstacles that may crop up.

I told my wife to get me a bottle of Vicks and some four-way cold tablets.

CHAPTER XII

THE SHOOTING OF BUCK HENSHAW

Buck and I used to do quite a bit of carousing together. He was an unusual specimen, sporting a flattopped haircut with a small-brimmed hat perched jauntily to one side and a face that looked like someone had slammed the door shut on it as he was hurrying through.

But, it was Buck Henshaw's eyes that were most unique. He had no tear ducts, and they stood brim full of water most of the time. When he was out in a brisk wind, he looked like he was on a crying jag of some kind.

As he jokingly said himself, "The only way I can tell if it's raining or not is by feel."

But he never ventured far without his beer, and this particular Sunday was no different.

During the previous night we'd had a nice four-inch early snowfall.

The snow clung to the trees and fences, stacked neatly on the tops of fence posts without the slightest breeze to dislodge it. I was out early, scooping off my sidewalk, stopping every once in a while to admire the untracked scenery.

Buck drove up along the curb and suggested we take in the picturesque landscape. That sounded like a fine idea. I leaned the shovel against the house, jumped in, and we cruised around the back roads, admiring and visiting. I took care of the bartending from Buck's twelve pack. Every so often we'd happen to spot a rabbit sitting along the roadside bank hiding in a tuft of grass or in a brambled-over fence corner.

"Buck, why don't we go back to my place and pick up my old single barrel twenty-gauge shotgun and plink a few rabbits for dinner?"

"Yea, I guess we could," he agreed, pulling into a farm driveway and backing around with his new snow tires giving firm traction as we headed back.

'Now, by damn, if we're gonna be messin' around with a gun, we better leave the beer alone. I don't like foolin' with a gun when I'm drinkin'."

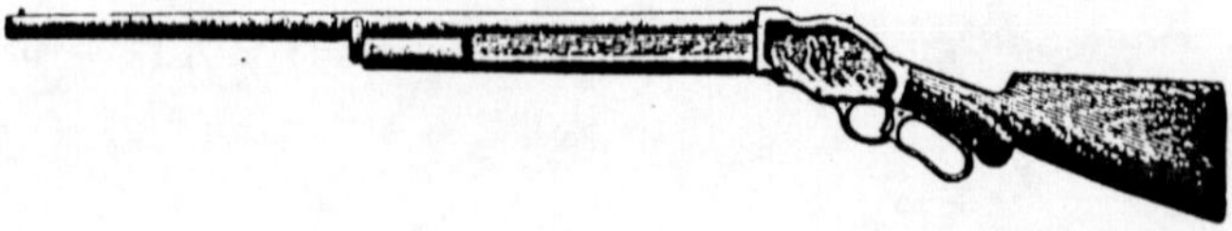

Buck was a fanatic on the subject of firearm safety, which was fine with me. I always tried to use common sense in that line, too; but Buck kind of went overboard with it.

"Okay," I said, "But a beer or two ain't gonna bother us that much. We'll play it real cool and not take any chances."

He agreed that'd be all right, but I noticed him give me a sideways glance when I popped the tab on a beer while we cruised around with the shotgun leaning against the seat between us.

Braking to a stop, Buck said, "There's one settin' on the side of the bank."

He pointed his finger and I leaned over, sighting along his arm, trying to get my eyes on that bunny.

"Where?" I can't spot him," I said.

"Gimme the gun, you're already blinder than a bat'."

As we got out of the car, the rabbit got nervous over all the activity and with an unhurried hop or two, disppeared over the crest of the bank.

Buck said, "He ain't goin' far, prob'bly stopped just over the hump."

There was a four-strand barbed wire fence along the road that we'd have to crawl through to get in the field. Buck handed me the gun, saying "Here, you hold this. I ain't chimbin' no fence with a gun in my hands!"

I stood there holding the gun, waiting for him to get on the other side.

Buck eyed how close the barbed wires were together and decided the best way was to crawl under. The snow was heavy and wet, and he got down on all fours.

It was at this time that I saw the opportunity for some fun. I reached down and got me a good fistful of snow, and pushed it into a nice solid little wet snowball.

'Long about this time Buck had gotten himself

caught on a barb. He was busy mumblin' something to himself about the heritage of fences in general, and this one in particular as he reached around back with one hand trying to free himself. Well, I figured I was just the one to give him a hand with that.

At the same time that I thumbed the hammer back on the shotgun, I let fly with my snowball, thumping Buck between his shoulder blades and dropping the hammer at the same time.

The timing was perfect. Buck went flat on his face, burrowing a furrow in the snow as he hollered, "Oh, dammit!!" He rolled over on his back, his watery eyes bigger than I'd ever seen them before, looking for blood on the snow.

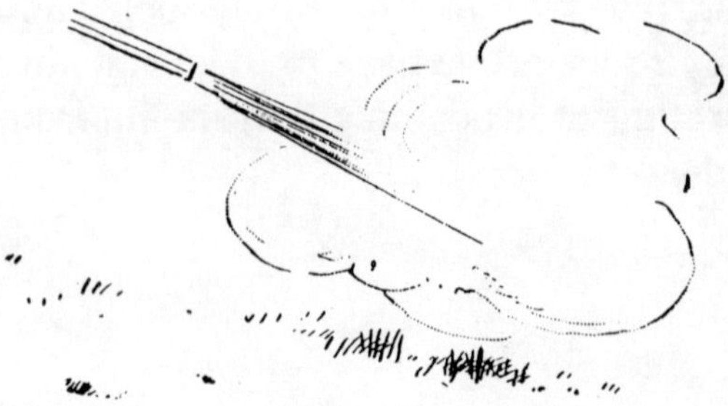

"Ya finally did it, didn'cha? Ya finally shot me! Oh, man!! I figured it'd happen someday!"

Well, I just plain got weak and had to lean up against the car for support. Buck sat up, swiveling his head from side to side in search of blood-stained snow and expecting the pain and shock to hit any second.

Seeing my reaction and how I needed the car for support what with all my laughin', it came to Buck what I'd done.

It was really luck that I had the shotgun shells in my pocket where he couldn't get to 'em. Not bein' able to shoot me, he had to content himself with callin' me every terrible name he could think of.

The name-callin' seemed to help 'cause after he did that for a while it seemed to calm him down and he could see the humor of it all.

Fact is, that kind of ended the rabbit huntin' for the day as we drove back to town and did a little celebrating of his coming back ta life from bein' shot dead.

CHAPTER XIII

PROBLEMS WITH THE TELEPHONE

Ludwig Swanson was a five-foot nine, wiry, and raw-boned man.

He was a true son of Sweden, having come to America in 1880 from his homeland.

Ludwig was nineteen years old when he got here from the old country, so had spoken Swedish for many years. It actually proved to be too many years since he never could quite get the hang of the new language facing him here in America. The two tongues became and remained hopelessly intermixed.

Ludwig married my Great Aunt Adra Peterson. Adra had one generation up on Ludwig since she had been born and raised in America. Her grasp of English was far better than his, of course.

Ludwig and Adra raised a family of seven children

there along the Skunk River on their little sixty-acre farm, losing only one of the babies to the grim reaper.

Life for the Swansons wasn't easy, but it was a good life, unbothered by the faster pace of most of life in America.

But change was to come, and not all of it to Ludwig's liking.

Electricity, for example, was far into the future for the Swansons, but the telephone wasn't. The telephone was right there and right then.

Ludwig had put up a pretty good fight against that telephone, but it was a losing battle. Even he realized that it would be just a matter of time and he would no longer be able to keep that awful machine out of his house.

Fate was not to be denied, and Ludwig eventually gave in and allowed one to be installed on the kitchen wall of their rambling one-story farm home.

Ludwig heard tell about the telephone and after giving it due consideration, he figured he needed no part of it. If Adra wanted to play that machine she could, but he sure wasn't gonna.

When the telephone rang during Ludwig's presence in the house, he simply ignored it as if it didn't exist. Adra did all the talking on that thing.

It was on a Saturday that Ludwig finally had to face his moment of truth.

It was the Swanson's going-to-town day for their supplies for the week. It was Saturday when the couple would take the eggs, butter, and cream into town in trade for coffee, sugar, tea, and other necessary items.

Ludwig had just gotten Adra loaded up into the buggy for that three-mile trek to town.

Now, getting Adra loaded up was no small accomplishment. It was, in fact, something of a project. You see, Adra had pretty much lost her maidenly form after hatching out seven children and it took a lot of heftin', strainin' and puffin' from both Adra and Lud to get her up into that buggy and sort of distributed a round there in the complaining buggy seat. It would have taken about three of Ludwigs to come up with the heft of one Adra.

It was during that breath-catchin-up moment between getting Adra loaded up and actually gettin' the team to movin' out that it occurred to Ludwig that he had forgotten to lock the kitchen door.

Since he had pretty much caught his breath again, Ludwig lightly leapt to the ground to get that little chore done before they left.

Ludwig was just turning the key in the latch when the lawful truth hit him. He could distinctly hear that telephone ringing there in the kitchen. There was no mistake about it. It was their ring, two shorts and a long. Ludwig wouldn't have admitted that he knew about that two shorts and a long, but he did. And that's exactly what was ringing there in the kitchen.

He stood there trying to figure out what to do. He hated that contraption with all his heart. He wanted nothing to do with it. But there it was; two shorts and a long.

He thought momentarily of running to help Adra out and down from the buggy, but what a struggle that would be. Not only would he be faced with that terrible chore, but when she got done talking on the machine, he'd have to load her back up again.

Ludwig's moment of truth had come, and he had to face it. HE HAD TO ANSWER THAT TELEPHONE!!

A thousand thoughts rushed through Ludwig's mind as he opened the door and went to stand in

front of that cursed oak box on the wall with all those odd-looking black things sticking out of it.

"Ring, Ring, R . . . . ing."

What to do?

"Ring, Ring, R . . . . ing."

This was the moment. This was the time that could no longer be denied.

Tentatively, Ludwig put his hand to that oak box and lifted the receiver just as he had seen Adra do.

"Yaah?" Unocustomed to having a male voice

answer, the caller asked, "Is this the Ludwig Swanson residence?"

"Yeah, shore, but dere iss nobody home hair now!"

So begain the real Americanization of Ludwig Swanson on his farm down along the Skunk River.

CHAPTER XIV

THE HOMECOMING

I had been away for some years. It came to me I was long overdue for a visit back home to the banks of the Skunk. Of late I had become lonesome for the old folks and my brother.

Also, I wanted to call on Edna Goff, the hard-handed school teacher of my youth and, if time permitted, I wanted to hunt up an old pal.

Why I so suddenly felt the need to come home at this late date, I can't really say. I'd made many good friends since leaving . . . . fine friends and business associates, but they still didn't seem to fill the void somehow. I had thought they did, but something was missing.

I had grown up in a small community with, I thought, rather dull and uninteresting people.

I told no one of my plans. I didn't want or expect a big hoopla made of it, just a quiet visit with a few who had been close to me and I to them.

Most importantly, of course, were my parents. I wanted to visit them most of all.

My, how glad they were to have me back home! We spoke of how long it had been. I asked how

they were and was glad to hear they had never been better. They wanted to know where and how and what I had been doing. I told them all and how sorry I was I hadn't written or come back sooner.

All was forgiven, as I knew it would be.

I thanked them over and over for all the love they

had given me and the encouragement that had so helped me to succeed. I had neglected that for far too many years.

They smiled and said such words were not necessary; they knew.

I asked of my favorite grandpa. I hadn't said good-bye to him when I left. I wanted to talk with him and set it right. I took my leave over to his place.

He was napping but woke and recognized me right off.

Heavens! How I had changed and grown, as is the way with youngsters! I told him he hadn't changed at all but was just the way I remembered him.

We sat in the grass by the big pine tree laughin' and reminiscing. I asked him if he recalled the slingshot he made for me from the fork of a sapling with rubber bands cut from a discarded inner tube from his Model A Ford and the leather rockholder he'd cut from the tongue of a wore-out work shoe.

My yes! He remembered it well, mainly 'cause of the windows I'd shot out of his buildings.

And we talked of the time he hired me to weed his strawberry patch. I'd done a poor job. Seemed I was too busy at the swimming hole and messin' around to stay with the job as I should have.

Yes, he knew I hadn't been out there long enough to have done a good job.

I told him of how disappointed I was when he'd paid me a quarter and let me start down the lane toward home, saying that was pay enough for the work I had done. Then, his calling me back, his deep-set blue eyes studying me and white mustache twitching as he handed me a DOLLAR . . . . . a dollar as big as a horse blanket, saying, "But that's what I think you're worth."

He brought up the time we went fishing and I thought I had a whopper hooked but it turned out to be a big mud turtle. I tugged and pulled until it came crawling up the bank toward me. I'd yelled, thrown the fishing pole into the air and had run for my life. We had a good laugh over that.

Such a nice long visit we had. Then I bid him good-bye, promising not to stay away so long. Even hinted I might soon be finished with my work and come home to stay.

I had to look up my brother. Lord! We had so much to talk of and remember. He was four years older than me. When we were growing up, he deviled and fed me more "bull" interspersed with enough valuable advice to keep me busy most of the time trying to sort out the wheat from the chaff.

Be that as it may, I can't conceive how I could have grown up without him. He was always pulling me out of scrapes and too-deep swimming holes.

After the usual inquiries into our immediate families, we fell to reminiscing about our growing up years on the farm. We'd reveled in bombarding each other with corncobs. Around the hog lots and cattle yard lay a profusion of cobs, handy missiles for boys to "konk" one another with.

In its natural state, a corncob is not a particularly dangerous thing to throw at anyone. But, let it lay and soak in mud and barnyard manure for a time and it will transform intself into a formidable weapon.

We had made a pact never to throw this type at each other. However, during one of our wars, he broke the pact as he always did when it favored him to do so. I got a heavy water-soaked, manure-cooked cob across the nose, temporarily putting me out of commission.

But, no matter, we laughed at those things, now.

Oh, I could write of so many things we talked of. It would fill too many pages. I told him my time was limited, that I wished to call on my old schoolteacher before heading back. He understood and we parted once more. I assured him I would come back again soon, when I could stay longer.

My next stop was Edna Goff's. I had hated her with a passion and I had prayed daily for her demise, prayed with the sure confidence of a youth forced to attend church and have the promise hammered into his head that "Whatever ye shall ask, so shall ye receive."

Of course I was terribly mistaken.

Edna Goff was a Godsend. The teachers I'd had before her were easy. They thought, and I let them think, they were teaching me something. In truth, it was a sham. During my seventh and eighth grades of school, I came under Edna's tutorage. The sham was over! She meant serious business!

Edna weighed two-hundred forty pounds. At the time, I thought of her as two-hundred forty pounds of meaness and fat, but later I was to discover her mind weighed fifty pounds, as did her heart.

Now, I took the opportunity to thank her for using the hard-handed teaching methods I had unknowingly forced her to use and how greatly I appreciated her time and trouble in saving me from being the next thing to an illiterate.

It was nice to visit with her, now after so many years. I thanked and praised her and said my farewell.

On leaving Edna's, I came across my old pal, Carl Anderson. Carl was the closest friend I'd ever had. We'd gone hunting and fishing together during our young years. Then we graduated from that to smoking and drinking and chasing girls.

Ah, the times we had, and now such a pleasant visit!

At last, I said, "Carl, I must go now. The sun is hot on my old bald head, I seem to tire so easily these days. You have a comfortable, cool place to rest and while away the time in friendly conversation. But for me, there is no shade, nor easy chair, to take my ease in."

But then, cemeteries are not meant for the comfort of visitors.

I bid you all a fond farwell.

EPILOGUE

After I left Carl's refuge from the cares of the world, I thought of the fun we'd had in the Skunk River valley as boys and young men. I thought of Axel Carlson's free light pole and the night we stole Kent Mills' homemade motorcycle; or did it steal us?

Then there was Frank Anderson and the day he blew his last dollar on a car that lasted him 'most half a day, and the love of a schoolteacher that has lasted 'bout a lifetime, now.

Life along the Skunk eventually brought all things, even Buck Henshaw gettin' gunshot and Ludwig Swanson answering the telephone.

Lots of those folks are gone now, but the river's still there.

Need a Gift?

For

• Shower • Birthday • Mother's Day •
• Anniversary • Christmas •

Turn Page For Order Form
(Order Now While Supply Lasts!)

TO ORDER COPIES OF

Skunk River

Anthology

Please send me ________ copies of **Skunk River Anthology** at at $9.95 each. (Make checks payable to **QUIXOTE PRESS.)**

Name ____

Street ____

City ____________ State ________ Zip Code ____

SEND ORDERS TO:

QUIXOTE PRESS
R.R. #4, Box 33B
Blvd. Station
Sioux City, Iowa 51109

TO ORDER COPIES OF

Skunk River

Anthology

Please send me ________ copies of **Skunk River Anthology** at $9.95 each. (Make checks payable to **QUIXOTE PRESS.)**

Name ____

Street ____

City ____________ State ________ Zip Code ____

SEND ORDERS TO:

QUIXOTE PRESS
R.R. #4, Box 33B
Blvd. Station
Sioux City, Iowa 51109

STRANGE FOLKS ALONG THE MISSISSIPPI
by Pat Wallace........................paperback $9.95

THE VANISHING OUTHOUSE OF IOWA
by Bruce Carlson......................paperback $9.95

THE VANISHING OUTHOUSE OF ILLINOIS
by Bruce Carlson......................paperback $9.95

THE VANISHING OUTHOUSE OF MINNESOTA
by Bruce Carlson......................paperback $9.95

THE VANISHING OUTHOUSE OF WISCONSIN
by Bruce Carlson......................paperback $9.95

MISSISSIPPI RIVER COOKIN' BOOK
by Bruce Carlson......................paperback $11.95

IOWA'S ROAD KILL COOKBOOK
by Bruce Carlson......................paperback $7.95

HITCH HIKING THE UPPER MIDWEST
by Bruce Carlson......................paperback $7.95

IOWA, THE LAND BETWEEN THE VOWELS
by Bruce Carlson......................paperback $9.95
(Farm Boy Stories From the Early 1900's)

GHOSTS OF SOUTHWEST MINNESOTA
by Ruth Hein..........................paperback $9.95

ME 'N WESLEY
by Bruce Carlson......................paperback $9.95
(Stories about the homemade toys that farm children made and played with around the turn of the century.)

SOUTH DAKOTA ROAD KILL COOKBOOK
by Bruce Carlson......................paperback $7.95

GHOSTS OF THE BLACK HILLS
by Tom Welch..........................paperback $9.95

Some Pretty Tame, But Kinda Funny Stories About Early DAKOTA LADIES-OF-THE-EVENING
by Tom Welch..........................paperback $9.95

Some Pretty Tame, But Kinda Funny Stories About Early IOWA LADIES-OF-THE EVENING
by Bruce Carlson........................paperback $9.95

Some Pretty Tame, But Kinda Funny Stories About Early ILLINOIS LADIES-OF-THE EVENING
by Bruce Carlson........................paperback $9.95

Some Pretty Tame, But Kinda Funny Stories About Early MINNESOTA LADIES-OF-THE-EVENING
by Bruce Carlson........................paperback $9.95

Some Pretty Tame, But Kinda Funny Stories About Early WISCONSIN LADIES-OF-THE-EVENING
by Bruce Carlson........................paperback $9.95

Some Pretty Tame, But Kinda Funny Stores About Early MISSOURI LADIES-OF-THE EVENING
by Bruce Carlson........................paperback $9.95

THE DAKOTA'S VANISHING OUTHOUSE
by Bruce Carlson........................paperback $9.95

ILLINOIS' ROAD KILL COOKBOOK
by Bruce Carlson........................paperback $7.95

OLD IOWA HOUSES, YOUNG LOVES
by Bruce Carlson........................paperback $9.95
(Stories about old houses in Iowa and young loves they have known.)

TERROR IN THE BLACK HILLS
by Dick Kennedy........................paperback $9.95

IOWA'S EARLY HOME REMEDIES
by 26 students at Wapello Elem. School....paperback $9.95

GHOSTS OF DOOR COUNTY, WISCONSIN
by Geri Rider........................paperback $9.95

THE VANISHING OUTHOUSE OF MISSOURI
by Bruce Carlson........................paperback $9.95

JACK KING VS. DETECTIVE MAC KENZIE
by N. Bell..............................paperback $9.95

RIVER SHARKS & SHENANIGANS
by N. Bell..............................paperback $9.95
(Tales of Riverboat gambling of years ago)

TALES OF HACKETT'S CREEK
by D. Titus.............................paperback $9.95
(1940's Mississippi River Kids)

LOST AND BURIED TREASURE OF THE MISSOURI
by N. Bell..............................paperback $9.95

ROMANCE ON BOARD
by H. Colby.............................paperback $9.95

UNSOLVED MYSTERIES OF THE MISSISSIPPI
by N. Bell..............................paperback $9.95

TALL TALES OF THE MISSISSIPPI RIVER
by D. Titus.............................paperback $9.95

TALL TALES OF THE MISSISSIPPI RIVER
by D. Titus.............................paperback $9.95

MAKIN' DO IN SOUTH DAKOTA
by various..............................paperback $9.95

TRICKS WE PLAYED IN IOWA
by various..............................paperback $9.95

CHILDREN OF THE RIVER
by various..............................paperback $9.95

LET'S GO DOWN TO THE RIVER 'N .....
by various..............................paperback $9.95

EARLY WISCONSIN HOME REMEDIES
by various..............................paperback $9.95

EARLY MISSOURI HOME REMEDIES
by various..............................paperback $9.95

MY VERY FIRST . . . . .
by various ....paperback $9.95

TRICKS WE PLAYED IN IOWA
by various ....paperback $9.95

101 WAYS FOR IOWANS TO "DO IN" THEIR NEIGHBOR'S PESKY DOG WITHOUT GETTING CAUGHT
by Bruce Carlson........................paperback $7.95

SOUTH DAKOTA ROAD KILL COOKBOOK
by Bruce Carlson........................paperback $7.95

A FIELD GUIDE TO IOWA'S CRITTERS
by Bruce Carlson........................paperback $7.95

A FIELD GUIDE TO MISSOURI'S CRITTERS
by Bruce Carlson........................paperback $7.95

MISSOURI'S ROADKILL COOKBOOK
by Bruce Carlson........................paperback $7.95

A FIELD GUIDE TO ILLINOIS' CRITTERS
by Bruce Carlson........................paperback $7.95

MINNESOTA'S ROADKILL COOKBOOK
by Bruce Carlson........................paperback $7.95

REVENGE OF THE ROADKILL
by Bruce Carlson........................paperback $7.95

THE MOTORIST'S FIELD GUIDE TO MIDWESTERN FARM EQUIPMENT
by Bruce Carlson........................paperback $7.95
(Misguided information as only a city slicker can give it.)

ILLINOIS' EARLY HOME REMEDIES
by various ....paperback $9.95

GUNSHOOTIN' WHISKEY DRINKIN', GIRL CHASIN' STORIES OUT OF THE OLD DAKOTA TERRITORY
by N. Bell.............................paperback $9.95